Into a New Day

Exploring a Baptist Journey
of Division, Diversity, and Dialogue

Into a New Day

Exploring a Baptist Journey
of Division, Diversity, and Dialogue

EDITOR
Kate Penfield

Smyth & Helwys Publishing, Inc.®
Macon, Georgia

ISBN 1-57312-049-9

Into a New Day
Exploring a Baptist Journey of Division, Diversity, and Dialogue

Editor
Kate Penfield

Copyright © 1997

Smyth & Helwys Publishing, Inc.
6316 Peake Road
Macon, Georgia 31210-3960
1-800-747-3016

Biblical quotations, unless otherwise noted, are from the
New Revised Standard Version of the Bible (NRSV).

The paper used in this publication
meets the minimum requirements of
American National Standard for Information Sciences—
Permanence of Paper for Printed Library Materials.
ANSI Z39.48–1984

Library of Congress Cataloging-in-Publication

Into a new day/
Exploring a Baptist journey of division, diversity, and dialogue
    editor, Kate Penfield.
    viii + 86 pp.   6" x 9" (15 x 23 cm.)
    Papers of a conference held Oct. 27-29, 1995,
    at the First Baptist Church in America.
    ISBN 1-57312-049-9   (alk. paper)
    1. Baptists—United States—History—Congresses.
    2. First Baptist Church (Providence, R.I.)—Anniversaries, etc.
    I. Penfield, Kate.
    BX6235.D58   1997
    286'.173—dc20   96-38530
                                                CIP

Contents

Until 1845 the movement among Baptists in the United States of America had been toward coordination and cooperation for the sake of common objectives. In that year Baptists split into northern and southern branches, primarily because of divergent positions on the issue of slavery. What united us, it would seem, had been overcome by what divided us.

One hundred and fifty years after that event, in October of 1995, a group of Baptists gathered in the Meeting House of the First Baptist Church in America, the church founded by Roger Williams in 1638, to revisit that history in order to discern the shape of our future. We named the conference "Division, Diversity, Dialogue: A Baptist Journey" because those words aptly describe where we have been in the last century and a half.

In those days leading up to the 1845 split, good faith efforts were made to hold the body together as people discerned at varying paces where the Spirit would lead concerning slavery. Now in these days Baptist bodies, once again bedeviled by threats to wholeness engendered by diverse understandings of the issues of our time, are making efforts to come together across lines that previously divided us.

In the midst of tearing tensions within existing Baptist bodies, there is the good news of dialogue between and among Southern Baptist and American Baptist sisters and brothers who formerly did not speak to one another. God is doing a new thing in new partnerships for mission, which perhaps may never eventuate in new configurations, but which make it possible for us to do the work to which God is calling us. Baptists are discovering that we need each other, not to make new denominations, but to get the job done.

The following pages represent the insights of eleven Baptists once separated into Southern and Northern, now united in conversation about cooperation for the sake of God's mission in this world. These papers presented at the Providence conference set the stage for the event, look back at our history, look forward to our future, and tell how to seize the moment.

As you read the words that follow, I urge you to consider today, with one eye on the past and the other on the future. God is doing a new thing. Do you not perceive it? Let us move into tomorrow in faith and hope that we are not doomed endlessly to repeat the fragmentations of yesterday, because God is leading us together into a new day the like of which we have not yet known, for the sake of this world that God so loves.

Kate Penfield

Welcome Home

Dwight Lundgren

Welcome to the First Baptist Church in America for this colloquium, "Division, Diversity, and Dialogue: A Baptist Journey."
I greet you on behalf of all our members. We trust that you will find
the occasion historically challenging and spiritually nourishing. We
also hope that when you leave you will be able to speak well of the
rich "Northern" hospitality you have experienced in our midst.

I want to begin this evening by sharing with you from a document the transcripts of which you may have read. It contains minutes
of a meeting that was held here at the Meeting House in 1845, April
24. Just the other day, Dr. Stanley Lemons was going through our
church archives. We thought all of the older ones were up at the
Rhode Island Historical Society, but he actually found the book of
the minutes of that meeting, and we are going to have them available
for you to see during the course of your weekend here. It's obviously
not a holy book. However, it's one thing to have photocopies, it's
another thing to have transcripts; but to suddenly have the book itself
before us is, I think, a wonderful, even a providential, occasion for us
here at First Baptist and I hope for you here this weekend.

I am not going to read all of the minutes. I will just read a por-
tion of a letter that was put on record and delivered to the meeting
that was held here that resulted in the movement toward separation
by the whole mission society. The words I want to read to you, it
seems to me, are particularly suggestive in terms of our time together
here this weekend and what God's will may be for us as the Spirit
moves in our hearts and minds and helps us to consider our future
witness as Baptists here in North America.

> In this spirit we have looked forward to this meeting of the
> Missionary Council to whom the Baptists of all the States
> entrusted their Missions with the heathen and with the earnest
> hope that we may desire great goods from your coming
> together; that our own views may be enlarged; our own faith
> increased and our own zeal for propagating the Gospel stimu-
> lated and made stronger.

The last few sentences of the letter include these words:

> And we offer our fervent prayers that your deliberations and doings may be guided by the spirit of all truth and that your meeting among us may be of lasting blessing to this church and to this community and may largely contribute to the advancement of Christ's kingdom among men.

And let us add in our lives and in the lives of our sisters and brothers in Christ and in the Baptist family throughout the United States.

Before I present Dr. Lemons, who will speak specifically about why it is appropriate for this meeting to be taking place here in the Meeting House, I want to just add two scriptural words that have been in my heart and mind as I have thought about our gathering and what this meeting is all about. First of all, a word from the story of Jacob and Esau in the thirty-third chapter of the book of Genesis.

We are all familiar with the story of Jacob at the Jabbock. After that altercation in the darkness, Jacob renames the place and says, "I have seen God. I have seen the face of God and survived." Immediately in the next chapter, Jacob meets Esau. After they have presented their gifts to one another and established themselves both in terms of remembering the past and desiring to move beyond it, Jacob says to Esau how delighted he is to see him and goes on to say, "For to see you is to see the face of God." And it is my prayer as we spend time together over this weekend that it will be a time in/through one another's hospitality, the workings of each other's hearts, minds, and testimonies that we will be able to say how good it has been to be together; for in looking into one another's faces we have seen the face of God.

Secondly, a word from the New Testament, from the twelfth chapter of the book of Hebrews. Let us be aware that if we did not remember the larger issue that was being discussed back in 1845—the issue of slavery and of human dignity understood in and through the lordship of Jesus Christ—that our proceedings as well as theirs would be just a matter of ecclesiastical rearrangement. There were larger issues at stake in 1845, and so I believe there are larger issues at stake in our day, other than who controls any particular Baptist group or which direction it should take.

I would like us to remember words from the twelfth chapter of Hebrews where the writer says—in referring to the breakdown in human relationships, the violent breakdown represented by the slaying of Abel by his brother Cain—"there is a blood that speaks better things, the blood of the sacrificed Lord, Jesus Christ." We must remember through that story the blood that was shed not just in the Civil War, but before that the blood of those who were slaves and whose lives were circumscribed and written off and whose lives became the issue and to a degree still are the issue. I trust that Christ's presence and his sacrifice will enlarge our considerations and our sense of what is at stake in our day and age and in terms of our stewardship and responsibility within the Baptist family; not just for ourselves, our polity, not just because of those memories from childhood that are dear to us, but the larger issue of the reach of Christ's kingdom and the unity of the whole human family so that we march together. Amen.

Words from the third chapter of Ephesians, "For I bow my knee to the father of every family in heaven and on earth that we may be strengthened in Christ's spirit." Even though this is a colloquium of a scholarly nature, I would like to invite us to unite our hearts and minds in prayer.

Gracious God, we thank you for the faithfulness of those who came before us, faithfulness not so much to their tradition or their heritage but faithfulness to the call of your sacrificial love in Jesus Christ, who lifts all into your presence by the power of his sacrifice and the love that it represents working in the midst of our history and in our hearts and our minds. We do not know the full meaning of our time together. We know what occupies our hearts and minds, but we pray that your spirit will rest upon us, that the work of your kingdom may be enlarged remembering the words of your servants who gathered here so many years ago. We pray that you will continue to "wrestle" with us in the darkness of our hearts, in the darkness of these days, in the darkness of the concerns of our nation that we may come forth from that darkness and look into one another's eyes and towards you and say, "How good it is to be together. We have looked into the face of God." This we ask in Christ's name. Amen.

Colonial Baptists as a Popular Movement

EDWIN S. GAUSTAD

In seventeenth-century America, one cannot readily make the case that Baptists constituted a populist movement. For the most part, Baptists in those early years were a beleaguered, withdrawn, illegal, persecuted sect. They grew haltingly, almost begrudgingly. By 1650—some forty years after Jamestown, some thirty years after Plymouth—the New World harbored a grand total of two Baptist churches: one in Providence, Rhode Island, and the other in nearby Newport. After that mid-century mark, growth continued to be modest—only enough to insure that schism would occur. For Baptists began quite early to manifest that enduring affliction of conflict and division. The Providence church suffered from the Six Principle (non-Calvinist) controversy, while the Newport church found itself embroiled in struggles with the Seventh-Day Baptists. Not much evidence of a sweeping populism springs forth in this first century of Baptist life in North America.

Yet, even as a negligble minority in an insecure colony, Baptists offered some hints of a populism that would later appear in fuller form. Two examples may be offered. First, Roger Williams paid heed to the most neglected and abused minority of all: namely, the American Indians. One could not be more "un-elite" or, for that day, politically incorrect than to come to the defense of the native American. This Williams did in his quarrel with Massachusetts authorities over their right to occupy the land without purchase from or mutual agreement with the Indians. And when he made his first permanent settlement in what would become Rhode Island, he carefully negotiated with the Indians for land at the headwaters of the Narragansett Bay. The Indians were here first. It was their land, and morally it could become English land not by conquest and occupation but only by compact and negotiation.

In his first book, *A Key into the Language of America*, published in London in 1643, Williams revealed more about New England's native population—their culture, language, and religion—than had heretofore been known, either in England or in America. More significantly, he displayed an understanding of and a sympathy for these men and women that marked Williams as a rare observer in the seventeenth century. He thought that the invading English had no reason to feel superior or vain in comparing themselves with the Indians. On the contrary, as Williams indicated in one of his modest poetic efforts,

> Boast not proud English, of thy birth & blood,
> Thy brother Indian is by birth a Good.
> Of one blood God made Him, and Thee, & All,
> As wise, as fair, as strong, as personall.

Even more pointedly, Williams, in a long-lost work, *Christenings Make not Christians*, displayed a respect for the integrity of the Indian so profound as to convince him that all efforts to convert the natives to Christianity were simply wrong. Forced conversion was no conversion at all, but a perversion of the inviolate sanctity of individual conscience. If one failed to distinguish between a voluntary and reflective acceptance of the gospel on the one hand from a compulsory and uncomprehending conformity to the "higher" religion on the other, then one had learned nothing from all the religious wars that had torn Europe apart for centuries. Or, in Williams's own more vigorous language,

> The not discerning of this truth hath let out the blood of thousands in civil combustions in all ages; and made the whore drunk, and the Earth drunk with the blood of the Saints and witnesses of Jesus.

In the most unpopular of causes, Roger Williams quite early offered a hint of a populism that would years later reach out to the disinherited and despised.

The second example from this early period is of a very different type: a man who published nothing, who graduated from no college (Williams was a graduate of Cambridge), who achieved no intellectual or social stature. Obadiah Holmes did not so much appeal to the masses as he represented them. He was of the people: a glassmaker, then later a farmer and a weaver, a preacher who never made his living from preaching. Like Williams, he rejected the official ecclesiastical structures that Massachusetts imposed, favoring a simple gospel simply—and freely—embraced. Like Williams, he fled from the Bay Colony's religious conformity to Rhode Island's religious liberty—some would say religious anarchy. Unlike Williams, he would, following his flight to Rhode Island, remain a Baptist for the rest of his life.

Also, during his remaining thirty or so years, he would offer a simple testimony to the work of God's grace in his own soul. Since the minister "has received freely of the Lord, so is he freely to give." And he must give without pretense or false sophistication, telling the old, old story in all its moving power. Preachers must be ever faithful to the biblical account, and not labor to concoct "a mission of their own brain." Most of all, the leader of a congregation must see to it that every member of that body also undertakes his or her own ministry. For the church consists of "a people called out of the world by the word and spirit of the Lord." This holy assembly must wait upon the Holy Spirit, keep its fellowship pure, break bread together, pray, serve, teach, and "prophesy one by one." All have talents given by God, and all are obliged to use those talents in behalf of God.

For Obadiah Holmes, the "priesthood of the believer" was no tired cliché, but a vibrant reality. He did not stand above the people, but in their very midst: to serve, not to command; to suffer, not to preen; to embrace, not to demean. Holmes presents a prototype of the Baptists who, by the thousands, would rally around that denominational flag in the nineteenth century. Men and women who, without pretense, read and believed their Bibles and stood ever ready to tell what God had done for them and was fully prepared to do for all those who confessed their sins and professed their faith—these were his spiritual descendants. Holmes is remembered (if at all) for being whipped in Boston Common in 1651 for carrying the Baptist message from Rhode Island back into Massachusetts. He deserves to be remembered as the "common man" who serves as a noble progenitor of countless other common men and women who found refuge in a simple gospel, simply told.

Baptist identity and Baptist destiny become much more clearly defined by the middle of the eighteenth century, by which time the number of Baptist churches had grown from 2 to 132. This was still not an astounding figure, when Anglicans in 1750 had 465 churches and Congregationalists 289. But the real difference was not so much statistical as it was the fact that Baptists were now in a "growth" mode, while Anglicans and Congregationalists (though they did not yet know it) would soon experience stagnation or decline. Baptists, no longer beleaguered, withdrawn, illegal, or persecuted, were now merely despised for a populism that seemed to threaten social stability and theological purity. What had happened to change the Baptists' outlook on the world and their active participation in that world?

In a word or two, what had happened was the Great Awakening, that outburst of religious passion and emotion that spread through much of colonial America in the middle of the eighteenth century. In New England, this resulted in the splitting of the Congregational establishment into pro-revivalist (New Light) and anti-revivalist (Old Light) factions. Many of the New Light churches eventually moved into the Baptist fold, the life and ministry of Isaac Backus serving as an excellent and powerful example of this significant migration. In the Middle Colonies, one of the important legacies of the Awakening, an itinerant ministry, spread freely, so that no new settlement was long without its own preacher—more often than not a Baptist one. In the South, Baptist New Lights challenged the formal Anglican establishment, reaching out to the common man and woman, both black and white.

To the religious elite everywhere, if there was anything worse than a despised and semi-stagnant sect, it was a despised and rapidly growing sect. Baptists now grew with frightening rapidity, raising their voices and flexing their muscles; thereby, they aroused an opposition seeking ways to stem this rising populist tide.

A Carolina Anglican, Charles Woodmason, ventured into the backcountry where the New Lights flourished to see if the rumors he had heard about these people were true. What he found convinced him that not only were all the rumors true, they had not told half the dismal story. It was true that the Baptists had grown, Woodmason conceded, and at a dizzying pace. But was society better off as a result? Not all at, the Anglican concluded. "There is not one Hogshead of Liquor less consum'd" since the arrival and spread of the Baptists. No tavern has been shut down; on the contrary, they have multiplied along with the "Fighting, Brawling, Gouging, Quarreling" found within. And among the Baptists, "the Holy ones of our New Israel," as Woodmason sarcastically called them, are "Riots, Frolics, Races, Games, Cards, Dice, Dances less frequent now than formerly?" Woodmason's answer, offered either with regret or glee, could only be strongly in the negative.

He offered similar negatives to the question whether "Lasciviousness, or Wantonness, Adultery or Fornication" were less evident since the "Arrival of these *Holy* persons." But what scandalized Woodmason most of all was the assumption by these Baptists that they were as good as anyone else. They based their religion not on the scholars of the church or the learned commentaries on scripture, but simply and merely and offensively on their own experiences!

People recited their experiences "in that Tabernacle Yonder to the Scandal of Religion and Insult of Common Sense." "And to heighten the Farce," one watched in amazement as "two or three fellows with fix'd Countenances and grave Looks" listened to "all this Nonsense for Hours together." What we have here in the backcountry, this angry and hopelessly biased Anglican concluded, was "a Sett of Mongrels under the Pretext of Religion" giving serious attention to nothing but "a String of Vile, cook'd up, Silly and Senseless Lyes." What Woodmason testified too, so fully and so unwittingly, was that the Baptists had become populists. The days of Anglican dominance, even in Virginia and Carolina, were numbered.

So the Great Awakening represented a first emancipation for Baptists in America; the Revolution a generation later constituted a second emancipation. Baptists were major participants in this nation's fight for freedom, as they had been in the Cromwellian uprising in England a century before. The Baptist pulpit was utilized in the cause of liberty—all liberty, political and religious. John Allen at the Second Baptist Church in Boston delivered in 1772 "An Oration on the Beauties of Liberty." These words were heard at a time when public opinion was still being marshaled: no outbreak of hostilities had yet occurred in Lexington or Concord; no Declaration of Independence had yet been written or voted on in Philadelphia.

So Allen's sermon, which proved enormously popular and went through rapid reprintings, helped to shape public opinion on behalf of the cause of independence from "English ministerial tyranny." But, as populist, Allen did not stop there. To fight for freedom from British cruelty implied a fight against all cruelty, against all forms of man's inhumanity to man. And that, in 1772, pointed unmistakably to slavery and the slave trade. "Have Christians lost all the tenderness of nature, the feelings of humanity," Allen incredulously asked, "when it comes to the moral horror of slavery?"

> Or have Ministers in silence forgot to show their people this iniquity? Or could they bear to see . . . nay, to feel their children rent from their arms, and see them bound in irons and banished to be Slaves! O killing thought!

Even worse was the engagement by Christians in "this bloody and inhuman Trade of Man-stealing and Slave-making." Baptist minister John Allen concluded in 1772 that "this unlawful, inhuman practice is a sure way for mankind to ruin America." Since New England was heavily involved in the slave trade, Allen, like Roger Williams before him, embraced the politically incorrect and the politically dangerous in order to defend the people—all the people.

As the young black poet and former slave Phillis Wheatley wrote in 1774, "In every human being, God has implanted a Principle, which we call Love of Freedom; it is impatient of Oppression and [it] Pants for Deliverance." In the Age of the American Revolution, the rhetoric of liberty had a way of spilling out beyond the bonds that purely political orators intended. All this talk of liberty—did it not mean liberty from every cruelty and every tyranny? Many thought so, especially as the oppression pertained to blacks and to women.

A populist gospel must necessarily be proclaimed to blacks, slave or free, and to women, slave or free. During the Revolution and for several years beyond, a Massachusetts itinerant Baptist labored in Virginia on behalf of religious liberty, on behalf of Jeffersonian democracy, on behalf of his own denomination, and on behalf of the enslaved black population. "The whole scene of slavery," John Leland wrote in 1790, "is pregnant with enormous evils. On the master's side, pride, haughtiness, domination, cruelty, deceit, and intolerance; and on the side of the slave, ignorance, servility, fraud, perfidy, and despair."

With so many evils attending the institution of slavery, the obvious question was why not get rid of it. "Would to Heaven this were done!" Leland exclaimed. But the practical problems, he recognized, were enormous with the value of Virginia's slaves being estimated as around eight million British pounds. From what private or public source could compensation of the owners on such a scale possibly come? Somewhat desperately, Leland clung to this hope: "It is the peculiarity of God to bring light out of darkness, good out of evil, order out of confusion."

One good that did emerge from all that evil was the turn of the black population, in overwhelming numbers, to the Baptist message. Drawn in part by a denomination that had much to say about freedom and that had no intimidating (white) hierarchy to challenge the independence of black churches, the African Americans also found the lack of sophistication—so abhored by Woodmason—a strong appeal. A simple gospel was accessible and intelligible to all. This was true of membership; it was likewise true of entrance into the ministry.

Among Baptists, black or white, the chief qualification for becoming a preacher was a demonstrated "gift" of proclaiming or exhorting in such a way as to draw a following and win approval. Such a gift, assumed to be God-given, was, therefore, more than a merely human talent; it was a divine sanction or call. When a slave named Simon manifested such a call, the Roanoke Baptist Association purchased his freedom in 1792 so that he might have full liberty to exercise his gift. A century later, two-thirds of all black Christians were Baptists.

Though colonial Baptists did not proclaim the equality of women in a manner that would become fashionable much later, they did encourage women to exercise their "gifts," including the gift of preaching or exhorting and praying in public. Martha Stearns, sister of the influential Virginia itinerant, Shubal Stearns, "on countless occasions," a contemporary reported, "melted a whole concourse into tears by prayers and exhortations." In the nineteenth century, Prudence Crandall of Seventh-Day Baptist heritage stood alone in Connecticut in trying to promote the education of black young ladies. Frustrated and blocked at every turn, she married a Baptist minister and moved out onto the Kansas and Illinois frontier. Like other evangelicals in the westward movement, Baptists leaned heavily on women for leadership in the local churches and especially the local Sunday Schools that often preceded the formation of congregations.

The final event of the eighteenth century that requires notice is the adoption of the U. S. Constitution in 1789 and of the Bill of Rights in 1791. These actions constitute the third emancipation of the Baptists, for now freedom of religion was more than a dissenter's cry of protest. It was built into the very foundation of the new nation itself. And should one ask what these constitutional provisions have to do with populism, the answer is "nearly everything." Groups that formerly had enjoyed great privilege now found themselves on an even footing in the competitive marketplace. Other groups that had suffered ostracism or worse now found themselves unshackled in the struggle to win the nation for Christ. Some denominations feared a full religious liberty, or approached it only tentatively. Others, notably the Baptists, Methodists, and Disciples, seized religious liberty as their very own charter of emancipation. For them, this newly guaranteed liberty became not so much a slogan as an ebullient way of life.

Voluntarism emerged as the hallmark of American religion, with optimism and confidence its dominant features. In the first half of the nineteenth century, it was widely assumed that an emancipated and uninhibited gospel could manifest a power never before witnessed by a needy world. Every ill in society could be reformed; the rapidly expanding American West could be redeemed; the kingdom of God lay just around the corner. The millennium, as William Miller and many others asserted, was not a vague and woolly idea, but an imminent and exciting reality. What lay just around the corner, most unhappily, was not triumph but tragedy.

Bibliography

Butterfield, Lyman. *Elder John Leland, Jeffersonian Itinerant.* Worcester: American Antiquarian Society, 1953.

Gaustad, Edwin S. *Liberty of Conscience: Roger Williams in America.* Grand Rapids MI: Eerdmans, 1991.

_____, ed. *Baptist Piety: The Last Will and Testimony of Obadiah Holmes.* Valley Forge PA: Judson Press, 1994.

Hatch, Nathan O. *The Democratization of American Christianity.* New Haven CT: Yale University Press, 1989.

McLoughlin, William G. *Isaac Backus and the American Pietistic Tradition.* Boston: Little, Brown, and Co., 1967.

McLoughlin, William G. *Soul Liberty: The Baptists' Struggles in New England, 1630-1833.* Hanover NH: Brown University Press, 1991.

Strane, Susan. *A Whole-Souled Woman: Prudence Crandall and the Education of Black Women.* New York: W. W. Norton, 1990.

Symbol of an Era
The General Missionary Convention and a National Vision

WILLIAM H. BRACKNEY

The first half of the nineteenth century represents for Baptists in the United States a time of unparalleled unity and cooperation. For more than three decades Baptist congregations and leaders exercised the full meaning of the associational principle, and the result was expansion in every sector of denominational life and a sense of denominational maturity. The symbol of the era was the periodic "Triennial Convention," which brought together the best of leadership and resources from the Northeast, the South, and the West.[1] But from its inception, there were powerful influences in the national gatherings that portended sectional disintegration.

The Reverend Morgan Edwards (1722–1795), esteemed pastor of the First Baptist Church, Philadelphia, may be credited with first suggesting a union of Baptists in America for the sake of enhanced mission and greater fellowship. He thought in 1770 that

> these means will not only be useful for receiving and returning intelligence, mutual advice, help, etc., but also for "knitting together" the several parts of the visible baptist church on the continent, as the parts of the natural body are by "joints and bands."[2]

Edwards' plan failed in its generation because of a lack of denominational maturity between Baptists in the South, a New England proclivity for regional autonomy, and a general reluctance to accept the dominance of the Philadelphia Association, of which Edwards was a part. Indeed, John Rippon (1751–1836), the English Baptist pastor and hymnist, through his *Baptist Annual Register*, went so far as to suggest in the 1790s that a union of Baptists on both sides of the Atlantic was desirable.[3] Strong local associational bonds, plus an expanding frontier experience, prevented the natural course of events from reaching any national expression in the eighteenth-century Baptist community.

The actual beginning of a unified national Baptist organization is found in other circumstances. Luther Rice (1783–1836), a young sea-swept Congregationalist missionary returned from India, thought that the idea was his. Along with Adoniram (1788–1845) and Ann Judson (1789–1826), Rice had converted to Baptist principles in 1812, and leaving the Judsons in the Orient, Rice returned to the United States to organize Baptists in support of foreign missions and to seek an appointment for himself. As for his master plan, Luther recalled it this way:

> While passing from Richmond to Petersburg in the stage an enlarged view of the business opened upon my contemplations. The plan which suggested itself to my mind, that of forming one principal society in each state, bearing the name of the state, and others in the same state, auxiliary to that; and by these large or state societies, delegates to be appointed to form one general society.[4]

Rice thus found it expedient to bypass the several associations—including the Philadelphia group—and create an entirely new network. Originally his concept was to build upon single-purpose voluntary societies that would form a triangle of relationships from the one national body to the many regional and local societies. The idea worked because the rallying point attracted great attention and did not immediately touch upon local or regional prejudices. Rice's dream came true on May 18, 1814, when the first session of the first convention opened at First Baptist church in Philadelphia.

Some writers have erroneously referred to this meeting as the first "triennial convention." On the contrary, the thirty-six delegates from eleven states and the District of Columbia agreed to organize the "General Missionary Convention of the Baptist Denomination in the United States of America, for Foreign Missions." Popularly known as the "General Missionary Convention," it had two important organizational components. First, a convention or general meeting of delegates was set up to organize the general plan of the work and give voice and vote to regular delegates once every three years. The convention was the vehicle for collecting contributions to the general missionary fund, upon which all efforts depended. Second was an implementing body, styled the "Baptist Board of Foreign Missions for the United States," which had the authority to transact business in the name of the convention between sessions.

Baptists differed greatly on an organizational scheme. William Staughton (1770–1829) originally favored a simple society that would resemble the British model that he had helped to organize at Kettering, England, twenty years earlier. Thomas Baldwin (1753–1826) and his New England friends likewise favored a society much like their own Massachusetts Baptist Missionary Society that still claimed their ultimate allegiance. In contrast, Luther Rice and Richard Furman (1755–1825) preferred the terminology "convention" because it carried a broad, nationalistic sense with it that transcended regional issues and united diverse factions. Furman, a Southerner, no doubt especially preferred a convention because of his masterful ability to blend opinions in large gatherings and to use his powers of oratory to move congregations. The terminology "convention" became for Baptists a symbol of unity amidst diversity of regions and states.

The first meeting of the General Missionary Convention lasted for six days and illustrated a geographical distribution that favored the Northeast. Philadelphia was chosen for the site of the meeting because of its ease of access by land or water and its proximity to both the North and the South. Although the nation's capital had been relocated to Washington, D.C., Philadelphia was still a principal city and enjoyed a military security during the hostilities of the Napoleonic Wars. Further, for Baptists, Philadelphia was an historic center in which a strong community of local churches existed in relative institutional prosperity. The Philadelphia Baptist Association also included a powerful ministerial elite, which at times created conflict.[5]

Two figures stood out from among all others in the formation of the convention and the implementation of its directives. Richard Furman of First Baptist, Charleston, a Revolutionary War hero and well-known preacher in the South, became the fount from which ideals and major principles emanated. Furman was a thoroughgoing nationalist who also articulated well the needs of his section. He dreamed of domestic (within the United States) evangelism and higher education for ministers, missionaries, and others interested in the "diffusion of knowledge and liberal science."

The other standout personality was thirty-one-year-old Luther Rice. Early in the convention sessions Rice acted as a continual staff resource and political organizer. He was appointed to the committee that drafted a constitution, and there is strong evidence of his hand in the recording of minutes and the management of debates. Almost all of the assignments following the session went to Luther: correspondence with appropriate churches and persons, organization of greater support for the effort, publication of minutes, and activities as principal agent of the board. Rice defined his role quite loosely, and he delighted in being the sole agent of the convention.

In the grand idealism of every initial meeting, the delegates left First Baptist, Philadelphia, with the poignancy of Furman's remarks impressed upon their minds and hearts. "Our delightful union," he mused,

> will never interfere with the independence of the churches, as [it] is entirely voluntary. . . . We have one Lord, one faith, one baptism; why should our ignorance of each other continue? Why prevent us from uniting in one common effort for the glory of the Son of God? At the present convention the sight of brethren who had never met each other before, and who a few months ago had never expected to meet on earth, afforded mutual and unutterable pleasure. It was as if the first interviews of heaven had been anticipated.[6]

In 1817 the first Triennial Convention was largely a replay of the 1814 meetings. The focus was still upon Philadelphia and the twin pillars of Richard Furman; Luther Rice became a triumvirate with William Staughton. Staughton brought to the corresponding secretaryship a transatlantic experience and a well-traveled personal history in the United States. He understood the South—having been a pastor there—he had traveled in the transappalachian West, and he had built a great congregation in Philadelphia. Moreover, Staughton had started in his home the first theological school among the American Baptists, which marked him as a leader among important young persons in the Middle States. His experience, coupled with Furman's reputation and Rice's indefatigable labor, suggested energetic opportunities ahead for the growing denomination.

Fifty-five delegates from fourteen states and Washington, D.C., gathered at the first triennial meeting of the General Missionary Convention, tackled an agenda that pointed to far-reaching changes in the work of the convention and the scope of Baptist work in the United States. Two changes were suggested for the constitution, namely that the purposes of the convention be enlarged to include home missions and education.

The third meeting of the General Missionary convention continued the Philadelphia tradition. In May 1820, once again the delegates convened in Sansom Street Church, Philadelphia, and once again the venerable Richard Furman presided over the opening session. Very shortly his close colleague from Virginia, Robert B. Semple (1769–1831), was chosen president, ensuring the all-important Southern Baptist linkage.

The name of the convention was expanded officially in 1820, to encompass the idea of "other important objects relating to the Redeemer's Kingdom." This was a permanent recognition of the expansion into home missions and education proposed in 1817. To the credit of Furman, a full article was added empowering the board to construct buildings and obtain a faculty for the soon-to-be educational institution. A salary was provided for the corresponding secretary, a clear recognition of the move to a more formal organizational status for the convention.[7] The board also authorized the establishment in Washington, D.C., of a college and theological school that focused the dream of Richard Furman. Importantly, the convention ceased to be a voluntary body in 1820.

The third Triennial Convention opened in April, 1823, in Washington, D.C., significantly in the nation's capital. Luther Rice and Obadiah Brown (1779–1852) intended to make the Baptist accomplishments in the new city a showplace for the General Missionary Convention. The new college buildings were well underway for all to observe; Rice had also arranged for publicity of the convention among U.S. Congressmen and members of the executive branch. The official publication of the convention, *The Latter Day Luminary*, had its headquarters in the District of Columbia, which Rice hoped would soon become the permanent home base of the General Missionary Convention. The attendance at the public meetings exceeded even Rice's estimates, and the assembly shifted from the Baptist church to the Presbyterian meetinghouse on F Street.

Among the highlights of this session was the presentation of the official charter for the convention, issued by the governor and legislature of the State of Pennsylvania. The document gave concrete expression to the aspirations of the founders and signaled public recognition of the corporate interests of Baptist learning and being desirous of founders and signaled public recognition of corporationists. "With a view of promoting religion and learning and being desirous of acquiring and enjoying the powers and immunities of a corporation," the document declared, "the said convention and their successors be . . . one body politic and corporate in law."[8] A memorable aspect of the Washington convention was a response to the proceedings from the president of the United States. President James Monroe's comments must have warmed the hearts of Baptists:

> Here there can be no oppression. Religion is free; industry, science, and the arts are encouraged, and vice punished. Wherever we take into view the present flourishing and happy condition of our country, mark its origin . . . we trace at once the cause from whence we derive our blessings. We see that we owe them to the freedom of our institutions.[9]

Mindful of eighteenth-century history, Monroe was thus paying a high compliment to Baptists for their historic advocacy of freedom of conscience and religious liberty. More important, probably, was the event itself. This was the first gathering of an American denominational body in the capital city and with which the nation's chief executive officially communicated.

The progressive euphoria of the first four General Missionary Convention meetings was tempered in the convention of 1826, which met in the Oliver Street Church in New York City. A combination of a serious economic downturn, plus a rising spirit of antimissionism in the Ohio Valley and parts of the Middle Atlantic states, created havoc with the anticipated receipts of the convention. To make matters worse, Columbian College had become a burden for the convention, with rising expenses, unpaid pledges of financial support, and real estate speculation that failed.

Ultimately, the convention decided to turn back the clock, revert to a single purpose organization, and remove itself from nonmissionary projects. An old show of Yankee autonomy, plus the protectionism afforded to both the newly created Newton Theological Institution and the venerable Massachusetts Baptist Missionary Society, caused great anxiety for the Boston clan that rose to prominence. The *Luminary*, first national Baptist periodical, was discontinued. By the mid-1820s, Baptist regionalism was beginning to exact a toll on the national vision.[10]

As the convention returned again to Philadelphia, every attempt was made in 1829 to achieve unity in the midst of growing diversity.

The fifty-six delegates reelected Robert Semple of Virginia as president and Lucius Bolles (1779–1844) of Salem, Massachusetts, as corresponding secretary. To placate those who still supported Columbian College, the convention nominated fifty persons for selection to the college board of trustees. In view of the ten Baptist state conventions formed in various sections, the delegates agreed to promote such organizations in each state, on the proviso that these bodies would be auxiliary to the General Convention and send funds and statistical reports to the corresponding secretary.

The national vision of the convention was again sharpened by a proposal from the Hudson River (New York) Baptist Association to keep alive the principles of unity and cooperation by forming an "American Baptist convention for General Purposes." "We feel impressed . . . that the time has arrived when we should have some regularly constituted bond or center of union, towards which as a denomination we might look," the New Yorkers reasoned. In their minds, support for foreign missions was not the sole value of a national organization; fellowship and visible unity were also important.[11] In response, it was decided to restyle the title of the convention to be the "Baptist General Convention" with an aim to promote foreign missions and "other important objects relating to the Redeemer's Kingdom."

Compromise had won the day in 1829, and, to no one's surprise, the next meeting was held in New York City. An editor noted of the seventh Triennial Convention meetings in 1832: "The session was peculiarly harmonious and important . . . the meetings for devotion were attended in a spirit of humility, ardor, and love."[12] The rancor of the previous sessions had passed, and so had the anxieties over Columbian College, which had become an independent institution. One hundred twenty-two delegates registered for this convention, held at Oliver Street Church in New York City, almost double the previous high mark; this in spite of the failure of the two designated speakers to attend the meeting due to ill health. The success of the meetings was due in no small measure to the substitute efforts of host pastor and convention president, Spencer H. Cone (1785–1855), who signaled a new generation of leaders.

The focus in 1832 was upon the mission fields themselves, and this strategy worked well in unifying the Baptist community. An observer noted that tears dropped from many a veteran's eyes when

Burma, Africa, France, and the Western frontier were depicted as the scenes of missionary endeavor. The emotional reports led to generous responses when the missionary offerings were made, which allowed for advances in the program of the next year. Since the political situation in the Far East and elsewhere had improved considerably from the 1820s, many new plans were laid for overseas stations, and the recruitment effort for new missionaries was stepped up. A "free conference on foreign missions" during the second session helped to rally support for a host of endeavors.

On the third day of the 1832 convention meetings an event of signal importance occurred between sessions. More than one hundred clergymen, most of whom were delegates to the Triennial, walked several blocks to the Mulberry Street Baptist Church where discussion led to the formation of the American Baptist Home Mission Society. Focused upon North America, this single-purpose organization was the genius of John Mason Peck (1789–1857) of Rock Spring, Illinois, and Jonathan Going (1786–1844) of Worcester, Massachusetts. These two men saw that the task of domestic missions was too large for the Massachusetts Society and that the principal interest of the General Missionary Convention was "foreign" missions. With the establishment of the Home Mission Society, Baptists in the United States had two national mission organizations to symbolize their unity.[13]

Although Southern leaders had presided over most of the activities of the General Missionary Convention, the meeting itself was not held in a Southern city until 1835. This was due partly to the difficulty of travel and partly to the primitive state of the Baptist organization in the South until the 1830s. Richmond, Virginia, was the obvious meeting choice, mainly because of the premier leadership of the First Baptist Church in supporting foreign missions: one of the first auxiliary societies was organized there in 1814, and the first black missionary was certified by that board. The 135 delegates present at roll call on the twenty-ninth of April demonstrated that travel from as far as Maine was no longer an obstacle for those committed to the missionary enterprise.

Something of the international vision of John Rippon was recovered during the Richmond meetings when Francis A. Cox (1793–1853) and James Hoby (1788–1871) of London, England, were welcomed with the right hand of fellowship to the convention. Cox and

Hoby were official fraternal delegates of the English Baptist Missionary Society who were sent to the United States to travel and to discover the nature of Christianity in the former colonies. Their official report in Richmond indicated substantial growth in Baptist churches in Britain and increased support for missionary endeavor. That these two would have any interest in the Baptist General Missionary Convention is a testimony to the admixture of American and British missionaries on many fields around the world.

There were definite signs of organizational maturity in the convention. One was to authorize an official history of its work at these sessions. Perhaps impressed with the record of the London Society or with its own ever-broadening purposes, the officers felt obliged to recapture the great moments and personalities of the first quarter century of work. They realized that the story of the Triennial Convention was also the story of a fragile unity of the Baptist movement in America. Unfortunately, the capable author of the book, James D. Knowles (1798–1838) of Newton, Massachusetts, died prematurely before the project could be completed, and the story was delayed until after the General Missionary Convention had been dissolved altogether.

Another mark of a more formal organization was the board's recommendation to hire a second corresponding secretary. Lucius Bolles, the present officer, reported that his duties included office management, consultation with personnel, supervision of fields, counsel to officers, and editorial work for the *American Baptist Magazine*—all of which was too much for one person. To make more efficient their enterprise, the board hired a second secretary in 1835 and created the first cabinet "for deliberate consultation and mature counsels."[14]

The grand plans laid at the Richmond convention were slowed in New York in 1838. Although in excess of $60,000 had come into the treasury in 1837–1838 alone, expenditures outstripped receipts by $44,500. Good work had been accomplished to be sure. Numerous missionaries had been commissioned in the period between 1835 and 1838; 38 churches with about 1,650 members and about 500 baptisms were reported in 1837–1838 alone; and the number of heathen languages into which Christian literature had been translated totaled fifteen.[15]

Nationally and internationally, American Baptists had much to applaud . . . and much to ponder in the midst of change. The two primary divisions of the United States in 1814—the North and the South—had become three with the West by the 1830s. Cities had grown up along the Ohio and Mississippi Rivers and across the hinterlands. The Baptist growth on the frontier was dramatic, and new associations sprang up throughout the region. More vivid were the population changes within the sections. In the Northwest, new immigrants settled in ethnically conscious communities; one of the formidable tasks of the Home Mission Society was relating to the Swedish, German, and Danish-Norwegian congregations.[16] In the cities of the Northeast and the counties of the northern border states substantial communities of African-Americans joined the Baptist movement.[17] From New England to Philadelphia and St. Louis, women organized for various Baptist missionary causes and made their voices heard. The grass-roots constituency that the Baptist General Convention represented in 1840 was profoundly variegated from what it had been three decades earlier. The political sectionalism that came to dominate the work of decision-making in the convention followed short-term national trends but obscured the social realities of the longer term future.

Whatever the national trends were, the Baptist community was conservative in its outlook, and this was evinced at the ninth triennial convention in New York in 1838 and later at the tenth gathering in Baltimore in 1841. The second largest attendance in the history of the convention—320—was experienced in Maryland's port city, in part because of the beautiful weather from April 28 to May 4, and in part because of the ease of travel. For the first time, delegates from a number of locations in the South and West were registered, and the convention was considered genuinely regionally representative.

In Baltimore, it can rightly be said that the General Missionary Convention entered a new era of leadership. With the election of William Bullein Johnson (1782–1862) of South Carolina as president and the deepening involvement of Francis Wayland, this new generation exhibited less of a national vision and more of a sectional interest. In 1841 Johnson initiated his tenure with a concern for harmony in deliberation and a respect for the convention process. Two important organizational changes occurred. The first change was to increase membership on the board to include eighteen vice-presidents, one from each member state. For the first time in 1841, however, the vice-presidents were elected by state in addition to the managers, which brought the board membership to sixty, counting the board and convention presidents. As of 1841, the board was to number more than the original attendance at the first meeting of the General Missionary Convention in 1814![18] Many argued that state representation in the board offices made certain the accountability of the states for board actions and vice versa.

A second change, however, somewhat nullified that impression and evinced again the regional undercurrent. A committee chaired by Nathaniel Kendrick (1777–1845) of upstate New York recommended the designation of a fifteen-member "Acting Board," which would enact the business of the board between its meetings. The Acting Board would be residents of Boston (the seat of the board), and only seven would be required for a quorum. Thus, in one resolution the convention reduced its administrative process to a group of seven Bostonians acting upon the advice of three salaried secretaries, who also resided in Boston. As it turned out, the fifteen chosen for the Acting Board were pastors in the greater Boston vicinity, leaders in the Massachusetts Baptist Convention and the Newton Theological Institution. A few Southerners left Baltimore grumbling over the reorganization of the convention and the reduction of its administration to a coterie of Bostonians.

Before the next meeting of the General Missionary Convention, many ominous external events transpired, mostly over the issue of slavery. Baptists in the North organized an antislavery convention and met regularly; several associations north and south passed opposing resolutions on the matter; editorials in prominent Baptist publications appeared in which strong regional positions were advocated. The great denominational compromise on the subject of slavery, which occurred during this period, was this: Baptist church delegates agreed that the Baltimore convention had no right to interfere in the matter and that union was more important than sectional jealousies. But such talk of union was disquieted by the continuing dialogue and actions within the board.

As 460 delegates traveled to the city of Philadelphia for the 1844 Triennial meetings, all realized to one degree or another that the slavery issue could destroy their unity as a convention. Many of the Northern delegates were participants in antislavery societies, and most of the Southerners entertained thoughts of seceding from convention membership. Symbolically, this convention, to be the last, was held in the meetinghouse in which the first organizing session of the General Missionary Convention had been held in 1814. Some of the Philadelphians hoped that the symbolism of the ambience would restore some of the lost harmony and vision. They were wrong. Owing to the declined renomination of President Johnson, the convention decided upon the leadership of Francis Wayland (1796–1865) of Providence, Rhode Island, who, though he opposed slavery in speeches and in print, was seen to represent a balanced opinion.

The postscript on the national Baptist organization was written at First Baptist Church in Providence, Rhode Island, April 30 to May 2, 1845. Under the watchful eye of President Wayland, several important realizations were reached. First, the predominantly northeastern nature of the Board of Managers was solidified. Of the twenty-six managers, ten were present, only one of whom, James B. Taylor (1804–1871) of Richmond, Virginia, was a Southerner. Prominent New York state pastors had joined the solid phalanx of eastern Massachusetts pastors to comprise both the managers and the Acting Board. Presumably all of these gentlemen were antislave in general perspective. One of the last prominent Southern board members, Jeremiah Bell Jeter (1802–1880), resigned from the Committee on European and African Missions, in absentia.[19]

Second, the Board of Managers was painfully reminded of its unacceptable indebtedness, now in excess of $40,000. An audit committee had examined the books and concluded the problem was too little income. A blue ribbon committee headed by Deacon William Colgate of New York City urged a new plan of individual memberships that would be the hallmark of the succeeding Union. The Committee on Agencies also recognized that field agents had successfully canvassed the Northern and Western states, where church visitations had ceased, except for the furloughed missionary Eugenio Kincaid (1797–1883), who focused on Kentucky and Tennessee.

The third realization was that the basic constitutional makeup of the convention needed to be revised. The Special Committee to deal with the Alabama Baptist Convention question conceded that since the question of slaveholding created a dilemma of conscience for some Northerners, the convention itself would have to decide on the appointment of slaveholding interests. President Wayland and his colleagues must have realized by this time that any future meeting of the convention would surely sanction the position of its board, given the predominance of Northern delegates. While all the Baptists in good standing, north and south, were constitutionally eligible for all appointments of the board, the die was cast against those with proslave sentiments, and a political/social issue had overridden religious unity. Providence, then, was the final occasion for Baptists in a national forum to debate the relationship of moral principles and mission.

Epilogue

The epilogue of the General Missionary Convention history was written in the life of its successors. One year after what became the final meeting of the General Missionary Convention, Southern delegates gathered in Augusta, Georgia, to give birth to the Southern Baptist Convention. Its similarity to the old convention was unmistakable. The design was to promote foreign and domestic missions, it would function in the form of a triennial convention, and delegates were chosen on much the same basis as in the old convention.

The wording of the preamble and constitution were almost verbatim to their predecessors. Indeed, William Bullein Johnson, who had resigned from the convention's presidency in 1844, became the first president of the Southern Baptist Convention through 1849. The most significant change was that several boards of managers were elected for specific programmatic tasks, and each was entirely accountable to the convention. With a common regional ethos and consensus on matters political and religious, the Southern Baptist Convention was assured the solidarity that the old General Missionary Convention was denied. Also, if the Baptist penchant for democratic decision-making was best facilitated in the form of a convention, Southerners had learned an important lesson from Baptist history.

In the North, things went differently. In 1845, following the withdrawal of the Southern delegates, the Acting Board scrambled for new support from associations and developed specific changes in the bylaws to allow for a composition of life members. Rather than continuing with a conventional model, Northern leaders restricted constituency involvement further, and the "American Baptist Missionary Union" became a simple missionary society.[20]

Little did the one who composed the General Missionary Convention Board report for 1844 know that he could well be speaking for the nation as well as his denomination. His words were at once a prophecy and an epitaph for the convention:

> Thirty years have elapsed since our fathers assembled in this city to organize the Baptist General Convention. The generation now terminating has seen an eventful period throughout the Christian church. . . . of the thirty-two members present at the organization of the convention, only six survive. Many a standard bearer has fallen. Of the missionaries, also, many rest from their labours. We who survive . . . cannot review this history without the most solemn solicitude as to the amount of missionary work which will be done by American Baptists during the next thirty years. Few of us will survive the close of the generation on which we are about to enter. May we so devote ourselves to the great work assigned to us by our Master, that we shall give up our account with joy and not with grief.[21]

Notes

[1]A more elaborate analysis of the convention is found in my earlier article, "Triumph of the National Spirit: The Baptist Triennial Conventions 1814–1844," *American Baptist Quarterly*, 4:2 (June 1985): 165-83.

[2]Morgan Edwards, *Materials Toward a History of Baptist in Pennsylvania* (Philadelphia: Joseph Crukshank, 1770) 4.

[3]*The Baptist Annual Register*, 1790. Rippon dedicated his first issue to Baptists around the world.

[4]James B. Taylor, *Memoirs of Rev. Luther Rice: One of the First Missionaries to the East* (Baltimore: Armstrong and Berry, 1841) 146.

[5]Robert G. Torbet, *A Social History of the Philadelphia Baptist Association 1707–1940* (Philadelphia: Westbrook, 1944) 52.

[6]"Minutes of the General Convention," 1814.

[7]"Minutes of the Board," 1820–1823; see the organizational tendencies in David O. Moberg, *The Church as a Social Institution: The Sociology of American Religion* (Grand Rapids MI: Baker Books, 1984) 118ff.

[8]"Minutes of the Convention," 1823.

[9]Ibid.

[10]This unhappy era is interpreted in Winthrop S. Hudson, "stumbling into disorder," *Foundations*, 1:2 (April 1958): 45-71.

[11]*Minutes of the Hudson River Baptist Association*, 1828.

[12]*American Baptist Magazine*, 12:6 (June 1832): 169.

[13]The story is told in Charles L. White, *A Century of Faith* (Philadelphia: Judson Press, 1932) 120-63.

[14]"Minutes of the Board," 1833.

[15]"Minutes of the Convention," 1841.

[16]White, 131-40.

[17]James M. Washington, *Frustrated Fellowship: The Black Baptist Quest for Social Power* (Macon GA: Mercer Universtiy Press, 1986) 23-47.

[18]"Minutes of the Convention," 1841.

[19]"Minutes of the Board," 1845.

[20]Historians should revisit the thesis that it was "mission" that provided a unifying principle for Baptists in the United States. Baptists, like other Protestant groups in the era, illustrated that sectionalism had a much more pervasive influence. As far as "mission" was concerned, it too would be divided by sections: J. Lewis Shuck (1812–1863) and Isaac McCoy (1784–1846) joined the Southern Baptists, while William Dean (1807–1885) and John Mason Peck (1789–1857) from the same foreign and domestic fields, respectively, remained with the Northern Baptists.

[21]"Minutes of the Board," 1844.

Francis Wayland
A Dramatic Monologue

Thomas R. McKibbens

Well, we are finally together again, and I could not be happier than to see us meet in this place, my church home and the city of my life work as president of Brown University for thirty-five years. When I came here to Brown in 1827, we were still together—North and South. I witnessed with great sadness our division in 1845. I grieved over our separation and the madness of the war that ensued. My friends, I never visited the South, but I had close and devoted friends there. I came to know them in my work as pastor of the First Baptist Church in Boston and later as president of Brown. At our meetings of the Triennial Convention, I came to know and love them as fellow travelers along the gospel road. This continual separation of people who should be one is a continuation of our great national tragedy.

Oh, don't get me wrong. The days of the Triennial Convention were not all sweetness and light. We had great debates and heated disagreements. In particular, I took on Luther Rice in the Triennial meeting of the Convention in New York in the spring of 1826. It was my considered opinion that Luther Rice was doing more harm than good to the cause of missions. I had great respect for the man's intentions, but I concluded that he had become so enamored with the raising of funds for the Columbian College in Washington that the cause of missions was being damaged. And after all, the very reason for our existence as a denomination was the cause of missions. But even after that great debate, we were still friends.

So our union, even in the days of the Triennial Convention, did not rest on common agreement as to priorities and strategies. Our union rested on something else. We believed some things in common that distinguished us from other Christians. Need I remind you of those things?

I

When Roger Williams established this colony, this church was founded on the belief in the absolute right of private judgment in all matters of religion. The scriptures were not given by God to a priesthood, to then be interpreted and shaped to their own understanding, and then retailed by the pennyworth to the people. On the contrary, we believe that the whole revelation of scripture, with all its abundance of blessing and its exceedingly great and precious promises, is a communication from God to every individual of the human race. We are all bound to study it and to govern our lives as we understand it. We are to determine for ourselves what is the will of God for us.[1]

With that view of individual responsibility, our view of the nature of the church is naturally somewhat peculiar and even suspect to those around us. Yet we have continued to hold to the view that every church is a perfectly independent community, under law to no one but him who is our Master, even Christ. This idea, throughout our history, has been deeply rooted in the mind of every individual and every church among us.

We have thousands of associations in the United States; but there is not one of them, however powerful, that would think of exercising control over the weakest or the most inconsiderable church. Should that be attempted, it is my judgment that the whole denomination should side with the church and withdraw from the association. No individual or single church among the Baptists can be controlled or dictated to by any ecclesiastical authority, be it a priesthood or an association or convention. No true Baptist will tolerate ecclesiastical tyranny over matters of conscience![2]

Closely allied to this belief is the conviction that the church should be wholly and absolutely independent of civil power. Just as no Baptist association, no matter how good the intention, can dictate to a single Baptist church in matters of conscience, so no civil authority, no matter how well-intentioned, can legislate in matters of conscience. The state can rightfully intercede when human rights are violated, but in matters that concern our relationship with God, the state has no jurisdiction. Thus the state must not prohibit or even annoy religion. If it favors one over another, if it restricts the exercise of any form of devotion, or in any manner interferes in the matter of religious belief or practice, it is stepping over the line of its rightful authority.

Such was the view of Roger Williams when he established this commonwealth with its fundamental principle of perfect freedom of religion; or, as he so well designated it, "soul liberty." I must admit that I have a high view of the Puritans who established themselves in this country. They were noble in their religious sentiments. We cannot help but respect people who will suffer the loss of all things rather than submit to religious persecution. But the truth is that they sought liberty of conscience only for themselves. They failed to generalize their principles and yield to others what they claimed as their own inalienable birthright. Hence, persecution became as rife on this side of the Atlantic as on the other.

Everyone knows the treatment Roger Williams received at their hands, to say nothing of Obadiah Holmes, John Clarke, and John Crandall. I have spoken myself with people in two New England states who have suffered the loss of goods and even imprisonment because they would not pay taxes for the support of the standing order.

Here, in Rhode Island, is the place to remember this peculiar glory of our Baptist heritage. We were the first to promote absolute religious freedom undefiled by any violation of the rights of conscience. This great belief was not only declared, but a government was established in conformity to it, at a time when there was not a square foot in this country where Baptists could, without molestation, worship God according to the dictates of their own conscience. And in a day when there was not a colony in America in which the charter of a Baptist college could have been obtained, Rhode Island College (now Brown University) was incorporated. True to their principles, the Baptists inserted a provision in the charter of the college, by which the various denominations then present in Rhode Island would have a voice in the government of the college.

These principles of the Baptists, which Roger Williams and John Clarke and others here in Rhode Island fleshed out in this little state, are now the glory of this great republic. These things Baptists in the North and South have held in common. Such being the facts known to all the world, have we any reason to be ashamed of our heritage? When the very principles for which they suffered are now acknowledged to lie at the foundation of all civil and religious liberty in our land, shall we hide our light under a bushel or blush to bear testimony for liberty? After having stood so long in the vanguard of that noble host who have contended for the inalienable rights of religious liberty and freedom of conscience, shall we furl our banners and retire ingloriously from the field? I know not what may be your answer, but I know what would have been the answer of Roger Williams and John Clarke, and I know what is my answer.

II

But now to that which divided us. In a word, slavery. The madness of slavery divided us. I call it a madness because that is my view of it. I know that I have been accused of being too kind to slaveholders. I refused to call them hard names, and I insisted on compassion and understanding for those who found themselves living in the midst of that terrible institution of slavery. My friend Richard Fuller of Baltimore, with whom I carried on a public correspondence over the subject of slavery, inherited over a hundred slaves from his father and was legally unable to free them. Was I to consider him a personification of Beelzebub because of his plight?

But there is more than sympathy involved. I also knew that the North was far from guiltless with regard to racial bigotry and even racial hatred. The North was not the promised land for people of African descent. There was a measure of freedom, but that measure was small indeed. People from African descent were systematically excluded from skilled jobs as well as from higher education.

In my day we were all familiar with the infamous and embarrassing case of Martin Delaney, for example. At the very height of my career as president of Brown, Martin Delaney was admitted to Harvard Medical School. But his admission was conditional. After graduation, he was expected to immigrate and practice medicine in Africa. But even with that condition to his acceptance, his presence in the classrooms of Harvard Medical School provoked a storm of protest from the white students. They claimed that racial integration would lower the value and prestige of their medical diplomas! They refused to attend classes with Martin Delaney.

To make matters even more embarrassing, the faculty capitulated on the basis of expediency and their commitment to academic excellence. So much for real freedom and racial harmony in the North. We here in the North had no reason to gloat over our racial attitudes.

If Northern urban economics had favored the introduction of slavery as plantation economics had, I feel certain that we would not only have employed that system, but would have defended it passionately with copious biblical quotations! We Baptist are always good about quoting the Bible![3]

So once we in the North get beyond feelings of superiority with regard to racial attitudes, what is left is common repentance. While political slavery has been rightfully destroyed, we have willingly embraced another form of slavery: We Baptists have become slaves to our separation. We have become slaves to our stereotypes. We have become slaves to our methods.

III

I am here tonight to propose what Frederick Douglas proposed to Abraham Lincoln in my day—namely, an emancipation proclamation. That proclamation, of course, did not automatically make freedom a reality. That required great struggle and sacrifice that continues to this day. It required a reordering of our national society.

But we can begin with a Baptist emancipation proclamation! We can declare our freedom from continued slavery to our separation. We can declare here at this consultation that while we may for a time still find it necessary to work within institutional structures that perpetuate our separation, we are one in spirit and one in our commitment to the principles that we inherit as Baptists. We will march under the same banner. And, we will struggle mightily to create ways in which organizational structures will facilitate our reunion.

You have, I understand, a new hero by the name of Kyle Ripkin, now famous, I understand, because of his endurance. I propose that along with a Baptist emancipation proclamation, we quietly determine in our own hearts to be the Kyle Ripkins of soul freedom. We take the field for soul freedom every day, year after year after year. We play our hearts out, and then get up the next day and do it all over again! If not us, who? If not now, when?

Notes

[1] Francis Wayland, *Principles and Practices of Baptist Churches* (New York: Sheldon & Co., 1867) 132.

[2] Francis Wayland, *Thoughts on the Missionary Organizations of the Baptist Denomination* (New York: Sheldon, Blakeman, & Co., 1859) 19-20.

[3] For a more complete account of the story of Martin Delaney, see Ronald Takaki, *A Different Mirror, A History of Multicultural America* (Boston: Little, Brown, & Co., 1993) 126-31.

Why Are We Here?

J. STANLEY LEMONS

W hy are we meeting here, here in the Meeting House of the First Baptist Church in America? The short answer is that we are here because the "last events" that fractured the General Missionary Convention of the Baptist Denomination—the so-called Triennial Convention—took place in this Meeting House on April 28 and May 1, 1845. On April 28, a special committee of the American Baptist Home Mission Society adopted a resolution saying,

> It is expedient that the members now forming the Society should hereafter act in separate organizations at the North and the South in promoting the objects which were originally contemplated by the Society.[1]

Also here on May 1 an earlier decision by the Acting Board of Foreign Missions to refuse appointment to a slaveholding applicant was ratified at the annual meeting of the American Baptist Board of Foreign Missions.[2] Consequently, the Baptists in the South quickly convened a convention of delegates in Augusta, Georgia, on May 8, which created the Southern Baptist Convention.

These events, of course, did not occur suddenly or without warning. They were only the *last* events, the "last straws." Let us look at the background and context for these final steps. In providing a longer answer to the question of "why are we here," let me state the general points that I want to make.

First, the Baptist denomination probably would have split anyway over an accumulation of reasons. (Given the polity of Baptists, splitting and splintering are practically descriptions of Baptists in general.)

Second, while the Baptist denomination had other sufficient reasons for dividing, the reason that it *did* split was the issue of slavery. Lest we Baptists feel that somehow we were particular failures for being unable to resolve that great issue, we ought to remember that the Methodists and Presbyterians blew apart over the same issue, and even the Quakers suffered a schism over their response to slavery.[3]

Everyone is aware of the Baptist penchant for division. Frankly, I would be a little alarmed if such turmoil were not part of the ongoing experience of Baptists. The absence of dispute might suggest that the vitality had gone out of the movement. Where there is controversy and even division, something is still felt to be vital and worth fighting about. Where there is peace and harmony, one might find a lack of commitment and the peace of the graveyard. Some issues may be truly beyond compromise, and slavery was one of them.

One of the earliest characteristics of Baptists was to divide over issues. Just consider the Baptists in seventeenth-century New England. By the end of the seventeenth century, New England had a total of ten small Baptist churches, and they came in at least three exclusive varieties. There were the Five-Principle Particular Baptists (e.g. First Baptist Church in Newport), General Six-Principle Baptists (e.g. First Baptist Church in Providence, Second Baptist in Newport), and Seventh-Day Baptists. (e.g. Newport). That was only the beginning.

In the nineteenth century, the national ranks of Baptist grew tremendously, and these ranks were swept by one controversy after another that produced several other denominations. From small beginnings in New England in the 1780s and 1790s, the Free Will Baptist movement in the North increased substantially in the 1820s and 1830s. For example, Free Will Baptist churches in Rhode Island became as numerous as those of the Regular Baptists by the 1840s. The issue of missions itself spawned antimissionary Baptist denominations such as the Primitive Baptists. The visions of William Miller, a Baptist, stirred people in the 1830s and 1840s, creating the Millerite movement, which became the Seventh-Day Adventist denomination. Other Baptists, calling themselves "Disciples," sought to overcome denominationalism by trying to emphasize only what they could find in the Scripture, and ended up in the 1830s creating still another denomination, the Disciples of Christ.[4]

Finally, there was that peculiar Baptist heresy called Landmarkism, which had its beginnings in the 1830s and made deep inroads into the thinking and attitudes of many Baptists in the South and Southwest.[5] Having failed to take over the Southern Baptist Convention, in 1905, more than 100 Landmark churches formed the American Baptist Association.[6] [A visitor to the First Baptist Church earlier this year impressed upon me the fact that his denomination had beaten the American Baptist Churches to the use of the name "American" Baptist.]

While all of these winds and crosscurrents ripped at Baptists, the mainstream of Baptists had its own problems. The General Missionary Convention of the Baptist Denomination had been formed in 1814 to support foreign missions, specifically the efforts of Adoniram Judson.[7] Subsequently, there were plans to found a Baptist college in Washington, D.C., to promote home missions, and to support a publishing and tract society. Southern delegates to the Triennial Convention wanted all of these activities to be under the direction of a central convention, but in 1826, the New England vision of a decentralized denomination triumphed. The Triennial Convention focused on foreign missions, and all of the activities of the denomination were carried out through different societies.

Instead of churches being part of a convention that oversaw all the enterprises, each church was a member of whatever society it chose to support. Home mission efforts were surrendered to the American Baptist Home Mission Society, organized in 1832; Columbian College floundered on its own; and the American Baptist Publication Society operated independently. Under these arrangements, Southern Baptists felt shortchanged and neglected. For example, the Home Mission Society focused its efforts in the West on such states as Illinois, Indiana, and Iowa, and neglected Southern areas such as Florida, Louisiana, and Arkansas. Moreover, all of the societies were dominated by Northerners, especially New Englanders, and nearly all meetings were held in the North so that Southerners could scarcely attend. In an attempt to meet Southern home mission needs, a Southern Baptist Home Mission Society was organized in 1839, but it failed by 1842.[8]

This difference in aspirations and visions of the Baptist denomination probably would have led to a split at some point. For one thing, the denomination was growing most rapidly in the South, and the imbalance of power and control was resented by Southerners. Something would have to be done eventually to redress the balance, but it is hard to imagine the New Englanders surrendering power or giving in to a vision that centralized control. Add to those matters the fact that Landmarkism had a tremendous impact in the South while having only a minor effect in the North, the advance of that controversy would have provided ample cause for a North-South division.

Moreover, by the 1840s, most of those men who had begun the Triennial Convention were gone, and a new generation had taken over. In a sense, the founders had failed to pass on their national vision of the Baptist denomination, and it was too feeble to overcome the sin of slavery.

Having said all of this, the second point is still true: the split was caused by the issue of slavery. The antislavery crusade had picked up steam in the 1830s, and by the 1840s, the North had thousands of abolitionist societies and organizations. On the other hand, the South had moved to an aggressive defense of slavery, even deeming it a "positive good." The issue could not be suppressed in Baptist ranks as abolitionist Baptists met in New York in April 1840 as the American Baptist Antislavery Convention, which established its own Foreign Provisional Missionary Committee.

A growing number of antislavery Baptists refused to contribute funds to the American Baptist Board of Foreign Missions because they did not want their money mingled with that from slaveholders. At the same time, in 1840 the Alabama Baptist Convention declared that it would withhold contributions from the Board of Foreign Missions unless it was assured that the board had no connection to abolitionism. The 1841 session of the Triennial Convention sought to paper over the growing strain by declaring its neutrality on the issue of slavery, and the board of the American Baptist Home Mission Society did the same.[9]

These declarations did nothing to halt the erosion of support for the home and foreign mission societies among Northerners. A rival American and Foreign Free Baptist Board of Foreign Missions was formed in Boston in 1843. When the Triennial Convention met again in 1844, the issue of slavery loomed larger. In an attempt to maintain a neutral stance, a resolution was adopted that said,

> Resolved that in cooperating together as members of this Convention in the work of Foreign Missions, we disclaim all sanction, either express or implied, whether of slavery or anti-slavery; but as individuals we are perfectly free to express and to promote, elsewhere our own views of these subjects in a Christian manner and spirit.[10]

The incumbent president of the convention, William B. Johnson, declined to serve another term; and Francis Wayland, president of

Brown University and a member of this church, was elected instead. Some historians have suggested that Johnson could see where events were headed, and he showed up at the Augusta convention in May 1845 with a draft constitution for the new Southern Baptist Convention.[11]

Despite resolutions of neutrality by the Triennial Convention, the boards of directors of both the Home Mission Society and the Board of Foreign Missions were opponents of slavery. In fact, the Acting Board of Foreign Missions were mostly from Boston, where the foreign mission society was located.[12] First, the Georgia State Convention asked the Home Mission Society to appoint a slave-owner as a home missionary; and in April 1844, the board declined to act on his application.[13] Then, in November 1844, the Alabama State Convention demanded of the foreign mission board if it would appoint a slaveowner. After delaying for four months, in February 1845, the Acting Board replied that if

> anyone should offer himself as a missionary having slaves and should insist on retaining them as his property, we could not appoint him. One thing is certain, we can never be a party to any arrangement which would imply approbation of slavery.[14]

The South reacted angrily to this response and began to make plans for their own convention.

The last chance to head this off came when the thirty-first annual meeting of the American Baptist Board of Foreign Missions gathered here in this Meeting House the last week of April 1845. Also being held here, as was the custom, during the same week, were the annual meetings of the American and Foreign Bible Society, the American Baptist Publication Society, and the American Baptist Home Mission Society.[15] Present, in addition to individuals from the First Baptist Church, were 319 delegates, including 37 members and officers of the Board of Foreign Missions.[16]

On April 28, the Home Mission Society proposed separate organizations for home missions. Then, on May 1, the Board of Foreign Missions ratified the decision of the Acting Board not to appoint any slaveowner; and exactly one week later, the Southern Baptist Convention was founded. So, those last actions, taken here 150 years ago, give us ground for returning here today.

Before ending, I must note that four of the fifteen members of the Acting Board of Foreign Missions had intimate connections to this old church. Both corresponding secretaries and two of the board members had been associated with First Baptist.

—Solomon Peck was baptized by this church on January 3, 1818; licensed to the ministry here in 1822; ordained here in 1823 before going to Boston in 1835 to become a corresponding secretary for the Foreign Mission Society.

—Robert E. Pattison was twice the pastor of this church, from 1830 to 1836, and again from 1840 to 1842, before joining his friend Peck as corresponding secretary.

—Barnas Sears was a member of this church from 1822 to 1827 while he was a student at Brown and at Newton Theological Institute, and he returned from 1856 to 1868 when he was president of Brown University.

—Finally, William Hague was pastor of this church between the two terms of Robert Pattison, from 1836 to 1840.

These, and the others of the Acting Board, were the ones who wrote that "we can never be a party to any arrangement which would imply approbation of slavery." If the Baptist denomination had to split, that was as good grounds for divorce as I can imagine.

Notes

[1]Quoted in Mary Burnham Putnam, *The Baptists and Slavery, 1840-1845* (Ann Arbor MI: G. Wahr, 1913) 51.

[2]"Minutes of the 31st Annual Meeting of the American Baptist Board of Foreign Missions, May 1, 1845," Archives, American Baptist Historical Society.

[3]The Methodist schism occurred at almost the same time (1844) as the Baptist rupture. The Presbyterians had already had a division in 1837 and 1838 over theological issues, but then both halves were shattered again by the slavery issue: "New School" Presbyterians in 1857 and "Old School" Presbyterians in 1861. While the Quakers had already eliminated slavery among their own members, they divided over how to deal with the issues of abolitionism and activism in their ranks. The Hicksite Quakers and the quiet, conservative Quakers "disowned" each other, beginning in 1828–1829.

[4]In addition, out of the frontier Baptist movement came the Christian Church and the Churches of Christ.

[5]One of the sponsors of the convocation was the William H. Whitsitt Baptist Heritage Society, a society that honors the memory of Whitsitt, who was a victim of the Landmark controversy at the Southern Baptist Theological Seminary in 1899.

[6]For a good discussion of antimissionary Baptists and Landmarkism, see H. Leon McBeth, *The Baptist Heritage: Four Centuries of Baptist Witness* (Nashville TN: Broadman, 1987) 371-77, 446-61. Regarding the Millerites, see Alice Felt Tyler, *Freedom's Ferment: Phases of American Social History from the Colonial Period to the Outbreak of the Civil War* (New York: Harper Torchbooks, 1962) 72-78; regarding the Disciples, see David Edwin Harrell, Jr., *Quest for a Christian America: The Disciples of Christ and American Society to 1866* (Nashville TN: Disciples of Christ Historical Society, 1966).

[7]A history of the Triennial Convention is found in William H. Brackney, "Triumph of the National Spirit: The Baptist Triennial Conventions, 1814-1844," *American Baptist Quarterly*, 4 (June 1985) 165-83.

[8]Robert Torbet, *A History of the Baptists* (Valley Forge PA: Judson Press, 1963) 288.

[9]See Brackney, 178, and Putnam, 21-27.

[10]"Minutes of the General Convention of the Baptist Denomination in the United States of America, for Foreign Missions," 1844, Archives, American Baptist Historical Society.

[11]Brackney, 179; McBeth, 389.

[12]The Triennial Convention had created a Board of Foreign Missions (which had up to sixty members) to carry out the purposes of the convention between its triennial meetings. Then it created the Acting Board of Foreign Missions (fifteen members) to conduct the operations of the Board of Foreign Missions between its meetings. In essence, a committee of fifteen Bostonians conducted the foreign missions operations of the General Missionary Convention of the Baptist Denomination. For details, see Brackney.

[13]Putnam, 38-42.

[14]"Minutes of the Acting Board, February 24, 1845," Archives, American Baptist Historical Society.

[15]Report of the Arrangements Committee to the First Baptist Church, "Minutes of the First Baptist Church" (Providence RI) May 22, 1845, Rhode Island Historical Society.

[16]Ibid.

Baptists in the South Searching for a Center

Bill J. Leonard

Several years ago I delivered lectures on Appalachian religion to a group of ministers in the region. When I finished the first presentation, and asked for questions, an older minister raised his hand. "Tell me something, Son," he said, "Do you think we'll ever go back to havin' two-week revivals again?" "I doubt it," I replied, "the times have changed." "For example, traveling to this meeting I could not help noticing all the satellite dishes sitting outside rural mountain houses. Now instead of a two-week revival, folks get 185 channels." Competing with satellite dishes makes the two-week revival, even in the South, a thing of the past.

Religion is changing in the South and throughout the American nation, and even the preachers know it. Survey after survey indicates that fewer and fewer religious Americans think of their primary religious identity in terms of a denominational identity. American churches are experiencing a significant transition in their organizational life, moving from one way of organizing religion—the denomination—to a variety of new styles.

Southern religious life illustrates those transitions. Distinctively Southern aspects of religious life are less discernable as the church moves toward the new century. Historian Samuel Hill, Jr. describes certain "common assumptions" or "conventional wisdom" regarding the nature of Southern religion. His list is instructive as we look to the future.

(1) Hill says, popular religion in the South generally is reflected in various styles of "conservative Protestantism." This includes more sectarian Pentecostal subgroups as well as denominationally oriented Methodists and Baptists.

(2) Hill writes that, "The biracial nature of historic Southern society is universally acknowledged as a crucial factor in the society's religious life, as much so as in any other aspect."[1] Hill and others have long documented the relationship between the South's "two cultures," black and white, from slavery through segregation to the civil rights era.[2]

(3) Certain religious forms—revivalistic, evangelical, pietistic, and experiential—have persisted in Southern churches throughout much of this century.

(4) Cultural and regional isolation or insulation has helped to shape the nature of religion in the region. Throughout much of the twentieth century, Southern culture provided something of a cocoon that insulated religion in the region.

(5) Hill suggests that the region has been characterized by what might be called a "pervasive evangelicalism," incorporating personal religious experience, biblical authority, and proselytizing missionary zeal.[3]

I would add that this style of Christianity also creates an environment in which sects can flourish and where religious radicalism and an establishment mentality exist side by side. Indeed, in the South there is a tendency toward both sectarian rhetoric and establishment institutionalism, religious people who talk like Democrats and act like Republicans. That is, many churches in the South talk the language of sectarianism—dissent, conscience, radical conversion, rigorous ethical code, millennial expectation—while at the same time identifying with establishment policies in relation to government, politics, education, and public morality. Beneath the rhetoric of dissent is a strong commitment toward preserving the cultural status quo.

Such a profile led historian Martin E. Marty, writing in the 1970s, to describe Southern Protestantism—especially the Southern Baptist Convention—as one of the most "intact" religious subcultures in modern America. Such intactness meant that a religious group exercised continuity with its past and provided a unifying sense of identity for its constituents in the present. In Marty's words, it revealed "regularities of behavior and consistent norms for evaluation."[4] Intactness meant that religious groups were held together by common cultural, organizational, and religious experiences.

Two decades later, however, scholars are now tracing the loss of regional intactness and the impact on broad national trends on Southern religious life and institutions. Sociologist Wade Clark Roof concludes that "no longer can an intact Southern religious culture be simply assumed."[5] Religion in the South has become more generically American in the last decade. The South, like other regions of the country, has been impacted by what might be called the

"Wal-Martization" of the American nation in which everything from shopping centers to rock videos contribute to a generic national culture that bears a homogeneity evident from coast to coast. In spite of this, Roof insists that "religion in Dixie is still characterized by high visibility, strong conservatism, and moral traditionalism."[6] He suggests that despite mass trends, "there is still a definite regional religious ethos and style" in the South.[7]

Thus we may say that religion in the contemporary South is shaped increasingly by national and global trends, while retaining a high degree of regional identity as well. Thus Southern religious life is in a state of transition if not major reorientation. Old traditions are being overtaken by powerful forces of regional, cultural, and theological pluralism—forces already impacting traditional religion in the South. In a real sense, therefore, we are living between the times, experiencing the end of one era and the beginning of another. If two-week revivals are no longer viable, how much longer will churches continue to promote revival meetings at all?

In many respects, Americans occupy a position not unlike that of our forebears at the beginning of the nineteenth century. Then, the forces of democracy and freedom reshaped irrevocably religious and political life in the new nation. Religious liberty brought an end to European-born ecclesiastical establishments, and churches, particularly on the American frontier, searched for new ways to organize themselves and fulfill their mission. The denomination became the chief method for organizing American churches. Cultural transition influenced theological revisionism as religious communities turned away from older emphases on divine sovereignty, predestination, and election to greater concern for free will, individualism, and democratic participation in everything from church government to personal salvation.

We are the heirs of that legacy, a legacy that seems increasingly less viable in our changing cultural situation and the challenge of secularism, pluralism, scholasticism, propositionalism, and modernity. Can we envision and reshape religious life as creatively as did those nineteenth-century Christians? What does this mean to the Southern Baptist Convention? My own analysis revolves around the following observations.

(1) The denominational center of the SBC was forged in the cultural ethos of the American South and the defeat in the Civil War, as

well as through participation in the "religion of the Lost Cause," and the prevailing racism of the region.

(2) The establishment of a denominational center protected the constituency from the dominance of numerous theological, regional, and popular subgroups that—implicitly or explicitly—sought to impose their sectarian agendas on the entire convention.

(3) Over a period of time the center shaped and was shaped by a denominational identity that created a programmatic mechanism for defining the convention and its cooperating churches.

(4) That programmatic center served as a safety valve that kept the Southern Baptist penchant for incessant controversy from evolving into full-blown schism.

(5) The center was built on and maintained by programmatic and statistical success. The success of denominational programs was evidence that the financial or ideological sacrifices necessary for its maintenance were worth the price.

(6) The centrist theology of the denomination was specific enough to be identifiably Baptist but general enough to allow for considerable regional and doctrinal diversity. At times, it was rhetorically orthodox and popularly heretical on the left and the right. While Baptists seemed consumed with maintaining theological correctness, and talked as if they were paragons of orthodoxy, their popular theology led them into heresy on such issues as justification, sanctification, and ecclesiology.

(7) The denominational center took many of its cues from the prevailing culture on such matters as race, corporate organization, and church/state relations.

(8) The centrist coalition was so obsessed with avoiding schism and retaining numerical strength that it sowed the seeds of its own demise. By retaining incompatible subgroups, the ultimate destruction of the old center was insured.

(9) The once impregnable center collapsed in the latter quarter of the twentieth century. While something called the Southern Baptist Convention continues to exist, it is merely a shell for an ever fragmenting assortment of subgroups each as yet incapable of reestablishing a new center for the denomination or for itself.

(10) The loss of a denominational center makes the SBC an intriguing case study in the demise or at least the remythologizing of American denominationalism in general.

Denominationalism involves the development of a center within a specific religious tradition or group. The denominationalizing tendency is concerned with consensus. Thus at least one important source of denominational centrism was based in Southern culture and the myths and mores of that peculiar region. It was indeed the *Southern* Baptist Convention.

For the SBC, the center was formed out of crisis—the split with Northern Baptists in 1845 over the slavery question and the subsequent defeat in the Civil War. In the aftermath of war, the denomination was charged with articulating an identity for the devastated churches, guiding them to combine limited resources toward collective endeavors—missions, education, publication—that they could not hope to accomplish alone.

This need for cooperation amid devastation was no doubt a factor in the decision to form a convention system somewhat more connectional than the earlier society method used by the Triennial Convention of Baptists north and south. Societies gave churches greater freedom of choice as to how to carry out programs and participate together. Churches and individuals could choose which society—home and foreign missions, seminary, publication, and the like—they preferred to support. Each society was autonomous without connectional relationship with any other. On the other hand, a convention system implied a greater connectedness among churches that had protected their autonomy tenaciously.

As the denomination evolved, strategies were developed for dealing with controversy. The SBC was composed of a variety of theological subgroups—Calvinists, modified Calvinists, modified Arminians, Landmarkists, and Texans. Doctrinal statements were specific enough to be peculiarly Baptist but general enough to provide a place for persons and groups across a wide theological spectrum. Subgroups were not permitted to impose their theological definitions on the entire denomination.

The fragmentation of the SBC began in 1979 with the beginning of the so-called "inerrancy controversy." Throughout the present denominational upheaval warring factions have divided, among other things, over the question of whether the debate was political or theological. During the early days of the crisis, moderates raged that the "takeover" was a grossly political effort to capture control of convention agencies. Fundamentalists hesitated to acknowledge that the issue involved politics, insisting that this was not a "takeover" but a theological "course correction." Both sides were correct and incorrect. Nothing in the SBC is or ever was done apart from both theology or politics.

Whatever one's position, few can deny that the SBC is changing irrevocably at every level of denominational life. While fundamentalists dominate the national convention, they remain unable to reestablish a denominational center or recreate a new sense of intactness. Rather, fragmentation characterizes every level of convention organization. While moderates lost, most remain within the denomination, unable to abandon the myth that the SBC imparted to them. Some still hope to restore their beloved convention, while others anticipate that the "pendulum will swing back" (it fell off around 1985). Still others refocus energy through new societies represented in the Alliance of Baptists and the Cooperative Baptist Fellowship, Smyth & Helwys Publishing, and innumerable seminaries now being formed.

Indeed, new or realigned institutions seem evident on every hand. Numerous Baptist universities and colleges—Baylor, Furman, Wake Forest, Stetson, and Samford—have renegotiated their relationships with their respective state Baptist conventions. Several of those state conventions are redefining their financial and cooperative relationships with the national denomination. Many congregations offer members a variety of options for funding fundamentalist- and moderate-based organizations. New identities are being formed organizationally and theologically.

Any discussion of the future of Christian community and institutions in the South cannot overlook the role of the so-called mega-churches already exercising a powerful ecclesiastical presence in the region. Mega-churches are those congregations that not only manifest a membership of several thousand persons, but also seek to provide a wide variety of ministries and specialized services for a diverse constituency. They are usually led by a charismatic-authority-figure-pastor, and are organized around specific marketing techniques. In a sense, mega-churches are mini-denominations offering through one congregation services—education, mission, publishing, small groups—that previously came through denominational networks. They are setting agendas for religious life throughout the American context.

This supply-side approach to the mission and ministry of the church portends the development of a kind of shopping center pragmatism in ecclesiastical life. It offers persons the opportunity to choose a church based on certain specialized services rendered, and develops ministries through effective marketing techniques. In the immediate future, Southern churches of all sizes will feel increasing pressure to accept or respond to the mega-church agenda, adapting ministries and services to specific constituencies, creating a variety of *ecclesiolae in ecclesia*—little churches within the church—to respond to the needs and preferences of specific subgroups. While this has often characterized the ministry of many Southern congregations, the specific marketing approach represents a new facet of church life and growth.

Modifications in ecclesiastical communities mean that a growing number of Southern churches will wear denominational affiliation more loosely than before. Indeed, Southern churches may give less attention to denominational structure than to regional and local configurations or confederations in which churches pick and choose what special missions, ministries, and activities they participate in or support financially. Collective—cooperative—mission funding will certainly become less viable for many churches. Instead they may choose to exercise a kind of line item veto, using limited resources to support certain specific mission endeavors that capture their attention. Missionary and benevolent organizations must learn to make their case more directly to local and regional religious groups rather than depending on national bureaucracies for their support. Denominationally funded agendas will only be one segment of an expanding number of mission-ministry activities that will vie for attention and funding from local and regional church bodies.

In light of changing organizational structures, perhaps one essential question is how will the churches pass on a tradition? Is there such a thing as generic Christianity cut off from the tradition of the church as well as from historical specificity? Are nondenominational, independent mega-churches able to pass on a tradition to succeeding generations? Or are they simply this year's new religious shopping mall, organized around a programmed obsolescence, bypassed by the next new mega-church offering newer and better shops and services to the next generation of converts/consumers?

Transitions in organizations also raise theological questions. Theological liberals and conservatives alike have lost or are losing their ability to provide meaningful response to the spiritual concerns of our time. For more than a century, liberalism and fundamentalism developed as two sides of the same enlightenment coin. Both utilized enlightenment rationalism to respond to modernity. Liberals promoted the historical-critical method and the effort to demythologize traditional religious ideas. Conservative evangelicals promoted Scottish Common Sense Realism and such recent ideas as creation science. Both have stressed the cognitive at the expense of the experiential, the rational at the expense of the spiritual. Both seem increasingly unable to address the needs of the times.

Robert Ferm, professor of religion at Middlebury College, wrote:

> The Christian faith and Christian identity are not as simple as many would have us believe. Issues posed in debates between "liberals" and "fundamentalists" are no longer significant ones.[8]

He suggests, insightfully, that much American Protestantism has distorted "the assumption that fundamentally the Christian faith is a distinctive understanding of human nature and human redemption."[9] He calls the contemporary church to consider the gospel as "testimony to weakness and power, to deprivation and strength, to a costly global view of our common salvation without platitudes or painless pap."[10] Theological debates are important but not always pertinent, particularly when they distract the church from the spirit and its mission in the world. In Christian history, when rationalism gets out of hand, a renewal of spirituality often follows. In a postenlightenment, postevangelical era, theologians, dogmaticians, rationalists, and propositionalists would do well to recognize this reality.

What does all this mean for the Baptists and other denominations? First, the Southern Baptist Convention established a powerful center that provided a sense of identity and purpose for its constituency. Grounded in Southern culture, the denominational program affirmed a theology specific enough to be identifiably Baptist but general enough to permit the presence of various theologically sectarian subgroups. That center is lost, and it will be a long time before it is reconfigured. Thus this denomination, like the original SBC, is in a time of transition. Those who want to hold on to something would do well to consider the benefits of the old society method from which the SBC was birthed.

A defacto society method is now evident across the SBC. Fundamentalist churches have long supported the idea by designating offerings to and away from selected institutions. Teaching them to do otherwise is a formidable challenge for the new owners of the SBC. Moderates are only now learning how to offer society options with many churches developing multiple choice plans by which members choose which SBC/CBF/local programs they wish to support. Churches forced to choose sides will simply split and add to the fragmentation. Best to give churches and individuals choices until new centers can coalesce. The divisions are so deep and the stakes so high, however, that society-based denominationalism may not be possible.

Second, the breakdown of programmatic identity punctuated the vast theological diversity evident throughout the convention. Moderates and fundamentalists are now discovering that developing theological consensus, even among themselves, is no easy matter. Those who want theological or political correctness to dominate the center or shape a new center should be prepared for continued controversy and division—the unending sectarianization of the Southern Baptist Convention. The new controversies will not be between SBC fundamentalists and moderates but between opposing or differing factions within multiplying ideological and ecclesiastical camps. Indeed, we should not expect the development of new centers any time soon, but anticipate the continuation of divisions relative to doctrine and practice, subgroup to subgroup.

Third, perhaps the real problem for the American denominational future involves the issue of identity. The denominational mechanisms that facilitated identity and enabled traditions to be passed on to succeeding generations are fast breaking apart or addressing only one of the multiple subgroups that still compose the SBC. Perhaps the most essential question is: When all is said and done, what will remain that is discernably, historically Baptist? We might also ask:

—How will fundamentalists and moderates pass on an identifiably Baptist tradition to their children?

—Will a kind of generic theological or political correctness, left and right, replace a sense of Baptistness, whatever that may be?

—How will local autonomy be sustained?

—What theology of baptism and the Supper will be passed on to a new generation?

—What mechanism for calling persons to ministry can be maintained?

—What will be the role of Baptist and non-Baptist educational institutions amid the rubble of theological education in the SBC?

In short, will SBC subgroups give their constituencies a place to stand that is or should be discernably and affirmatively Baptist?

Finally, a personal word. After more than a decade of painful controversy, many Baptists have learned to struggle with questions of what it means to be a Baptist and what it means to claim Christian vocation in a time of instability and transition. For some it has meant the rediscovery of one of the most significant and neglected aspects of our heritage: the dissenting tradition of the Baptists, the challenge to speak out even when in the minority. In times of stability or turmoil, that is a heritage worth retaining and passing on.

Notes

[1]Samuel S. Hill, ed., *Varieties of Southern Religious Experience* (Baton Rouge LA: Louisiana State University Press, 1980) 211.

[2]Samuel S. Hill, Jr., *Religion and the Solid South* (Nashville: Abingdon, 1972) 24-56.

[3]Hill, *Varieties of Southern Religious Experience*, 213.

[4]Martin E. Marty, "The Protestant Experience and Perspectives," *American Religious Values and the Future of America* (Philadelphia: Fortress, 1978) 40.

[5]Ibid.

[6]Wade Clark Roof, "Religious Change in the American South: The Case of the Unchurched," *Varieties of Southern Religious Experience*, 197.

[7]Ibid.

[8]Robert L. Ferm, *Piety, Purity, Plenty: Images of Protestantism in America* (Minneapolis: Fortress, 1991) 117.

[9]Ibid., 8.

[10]Ibid., 116.

Seizing the Moment

STAN HASTEY

> Do not remember the former things, or consider the things of
> old. I am about to do a new thing; now it springs forth, do you
> not perceive it? (Isa 43:18-19)

This colloquium has invited us to look at things past and ponder
future things. My objective is to challenge us to seize the present
moment, a *kairos* moment in Baptist history, by acknowledging both
the uniqueness of our history and heritage as well as the inadequacy
of a narrow denominationalism in the present context.

The Isaiah text chosen to provide the framework for these
thoughts and the discussion to follow seems especially appropriate for
this in-between, *kairos*, moment in our collective history as Baptists
from North and South. The historical setting for our Hebrew
ancestors was, of course, postexilic.

In his commentary on the text, Page H. Kelley observes:

> Israel's liberation from exile is presented . . . as a new exodus. .
> . . The prophet admonishes Israel to forget the *former things* (v.
> 18) and to turn her attention instead to the *new thing* which is
> about to spring forth (v. 19). The former things refer to the
> events surrounding the first exodus; the new thing is the immi-
> nent liberation of Israel from exile and the transformation of
> the wilderness into a paradise. The meaning of the prophet's
> admonition is that the wonders of the new exodus will be such
> as to cause the first exodus by comparison to pale into signif-
> icance.[1]

But what about this business of forgetting the past? Claus
Westermann offers this:

> Yet, this very thing, God's initial act of deliverance, "the former
> thing," "the thing of old," is, verse 18 appears to say, to be for-
> gotten, so tremendous and overwhelming is the new thing
> which Yahweh is now on the point of doing (v. 19). . . . But did
> Deutero-Isaiah really mean this utterance to say that God's new
> act and the new Exodus which is to be its result are so much to

overshadow his past act and the first Exodus as to cause them to be forgotten, obliterated by the new thing shortly to be expected? It would be very strange if he did. More than any other prophet, Deutero-Isaiah holds his nation to their traditions. Over and over again he most emphatically reminds them of God's mighty acts in their past. . . . It would therefore be very strange if here this same man were saying, "Forget what I did in former days, and consider it no more. . . ."

What he wants to say is rather, "Stop mournfully looking back and clinging to the past, and open your minds to the fact that a new, miraculous act of God lies ahead of you!"[2]

How does the experience of our Hebrew ancestors inform our present dilemma as Baptists? If it is true, to borrow Carlyle Marney's language, that "we Christians are a 'pilgrim people,' or we are dead," how do we Baptists approach the present journey?

In the Southern Baptist context specifically, the dislocation of recent years makes such questions necessary. In the aftermath of the termination of Southwestern Baptist Theological Seminary President Russell Dilday, a former faculty colleague of the deposed Dilday, Kenneth Chafin, wrote a poetic essay titled, "Baptists in Babylon," which included this conclusion:

But as Israel learned, all is not lost in captivity! We discover that God's presence is not limited to Jerusalem, or Nashville. Here God calls us to repent for making idols of the institutions we built where in pride and arrogance we bowed down and worshiped our own worldly successes. You can sing the Songs of Zion in a strange land, and it's easier to celebrate Christ's freedom in captivity than to learn "doublespeak" and conformity back home.[3]

Welcome to Babylon and the captivity!

Three years ago, Ralph H. Elliott wrote movingly of his own painful dislocation from Southern Baptist life more than three decades ago and his subsequent relocation in American Baptist life. Titled The "Genesis Controversy" and Continuity in Southern Baptist Chaos, Elliott's first person narrative is much more than the story of his firing thirty-three years ago as professor of Old Testament at Midwestern Baptist Theological Seminary.

Throughout the book, he makes a compelling case for the inter-connection of those events and the more recent—and now successfully completed—takeover of the Southern Baptist Convention by the same forces that ousted him. Yet Elliott was not then and is not now bitter about what happened to him, his family, and career. This is not to say there is no sadness in his account. Indeed, the subtitle of the book, *A Eulogy for a Great Tradition*, betrays a lingering grief over the lost potential of a body that once was referred to as the sleeping giant of American Protestantism.

Despite the value of such insights, however, what is to me most gripping about Elliott's book is the last chapter, "Introduction to the Larger Church." Using the theme of exile, he wrote:

> I made a wonderful discovery. Forced to live as a pilgrim in exile circumstances, I discovered that the new situation liberated me to clarify who I was and who I ought to be. I would covet for all exiles that, having made the discovery, they can praise God and celebrate the journey, even if the journey into exile was with a push.[4]

For Ralph Elliott, the journey led to the American Baptist churches and a teaching assignment at the old Crozer Theological Seminary in what he called "my introduction into a totally different world":

> The transition was an important one for me. It was both reluctant and painful, but it gave me a new family. It must be clearly understood that a sense of nostalgia for old roots in no way diminishes a sense of appreciation and thanksgiving for my new family. American Baptists have offered me opportunities I had neither merit nor other right to expect.[5]

Among these, beyond the Crozer faculty post, were the pastorates of prominent American Baptist congregations, as well as numerous highly visible opportunities in denominational service. Of particular significance to Elliott was American Baptists' active ecumenism and the opportunities afforded him to become acquainted with the larger church, so much so that he wrote:

> My life has been singularly blessed in the belated discovery that ecumenical oneness is the given nature of the church. I am pleased with the circumstances that delivered me from an isolationist and isolating Christianity into the richness of cooperative Christianity.[6]

Those of us involved in the significant transition now underway in Baptist life in this country and beyond have a lot to learn from Elliott's experience, particularly in light of the signs of denominational deterioration in the intervening years. This deterioration goes far beyond that of the Southern Baptist Convention. Denominational lines indeed are more blurred now than ever before. In Baptist churches everywhere, in congregations to be found all along the theological spectrum from fundamentalist to liberal, the sense of what it means to be Baptist is weak and growing ever weaker.

Among the reasons, beyond weariness with the Baptist battles that historically have characterized our denomination, is the simple reality that more and more non-Baptists are finding their way into Baptist churches of all types while more and more Baptists are joining congregations of other denominations. While on one level such an unmistakable loss of identity is to be lamented, the potential for what Elliott called "cooperative Christianity" has never been greater, surely a fact to be celebrated.

Within the movement known as the Alliance of Baptists, one of our seven founding principles is a commitment to "the larger body of Jesus Christ, expressed in various Christian traditions, and to a cooperation with believers everywhere in giving full expression to the gospel."

Not even the dislocation of the present moment, painful as it has been, can begin to compare with the sheer blessing of being relocated to a new and larger house. Perhaps the largest lesson our small movement of former Southern Baptists has learned in our still-brief existence is that we have spiritual kin in the larger denomination of God's people known as Baptists and, even more, within the whole church of God.

What some of us have even dared allow ourselves to begin to imagine during these past several years is the prospect of a new movement of Baptists unified around historic Baptist principles and committed to ecumenical Christianity. Such a movement even now is underway, seeking first to confess the barriers that have divided us, followed by the building of new bridges of understanding.

For now, it seems to me, the aim of such a movement is not establishing a new convention but the modest and more realistic end of collaborating in as many areas as we will allow our collective imagination to take us. These might include joint ventures in mission strategy, theological education, publishing houses, pension and insurance plans, and a renewed commitment to our common witness to religious liberty and peace and justice in the public arena.

Although it would be a safe assumption that such a movement would be progressive in its understanding of both the nature of divine revelation and the social order, those of us seeking to foster it need to beware of the trap of ideological exclusivity, lest it be doomed for practicing what we preach against. Such a movement must be open, for example, to a variety of theological and liturgical expressions and make plenty of room for seekers. After all, what is more contradictory to progressivism than a regressive spirit?

How feasible is such a movement? Some sociologists of religion, including our own Nancy Tatom Ammerman, answer that it is very feasible indeed. Citing the work of Stewart Clegg, *Modern Organizations: Organization Studies in the Postmodern World*, she has noted several categories indicating a move from "modern" organizations to "postmodern" ones.

In the category of "Activities," Ammerman has said:

> The modern organization was premised on mass production. Postmodern organization is premised on finding niches. . . . Just as we no longer assume that one kind of car will satisfy every taste, we can no longer assume that one set of programs can define a denomination. . . . Postmodern organizations assume diversity. And since they do not assume that everyone must buy the same product, they make room for pluralism.[7]

And under the category, "Relationships," she has noted:

> Modern organizations were large and centralized. Postmodern organizations are decentralized, flexible, relying on subcontracting and networks. Where organizations used to think that the only way to do something new was to create a new department within their centralized structure, postmodern organizations look for ways to accomplish new tasks by forming alliances.[8]

As applied to Baptist life in the waning years of this millennium and the dawning of the next, perhaps what all this means is that in spite of our proclivity to disorder, even division, God is not yet finished with us. Or, to return to our biblical text, perhaps we can begin to catch a glimpse of the "new thing" God is about in our time, in spite of our poor discernment and imperfect discipleship. Perhaps even, in the words of James Muilenburg concerning that prophetic word, we like Israel are being called "to turn from memory to hope, from the epochal events of the past to the even more decisive and redemptive events of the future."

Several years ago, Richard Groves, then-president of the Alliance of Baptists, told a story that captures our denominational dilemma about as well as any illustration I've heard. It is taken from Harry Emerson Fosdick's book, *The Secret of Victorious Living*, from which the following is quoted:

> Beethoven wrote music that could not adequately be rendered on the instruments of his time, music which, therefore, was in itself a prayer: "Give me instruments, create for me instruments so I can really be played." Suppose that you, devoutly believing in Beethoven, had heard the *C Minor Concerto* at its first rendition. You would have known, would you not, that that could not possibly be the end of the story; that though it might be a long time from Beethoven to Toscanini and the Philharmonic, yet the music would bring to pass at last an orchestra which would play it properly. So we, who deeply believe in Christ and hear his music being ruined . . . know that this is not the end of the story. Underline this in your faith; the future belongs to the music and not to these wretched, obsolete instruments.[9]

Notes

[1]Page H. Kelley, *The Broadman Bible Commentary*, vol. 5 (Nashville: Broadman, 1970) 312.

[2]Claus Westermann, *Isaiah 40-66: A Commentary* (Philadelphia: Westminster, 1969) 127-28.

[3]Ken Chafin, "Baptists in Babylon," *Baptists Today*, 16 June 1994, 4.

[4]Ralph Elliott, *The "Genesis Controversy" and Continuity in Southern Baptist Chaos* (Macon GA: Mercer University Press, 1992) 155.

[5]Ibid., 154-55.

[6]Ibid., 163.

[7]Nancy Tatom Ammerman, "SBC Moderates and the Making of a Postmodern Denomination," *Christian Century*, 22-29 September 1993, 896.

[8]Ibid., 897.

[9]Harry Emerson Fosdick, *The Secret of Victorious Living* (New York and London: Harper & Brothers, 1934) 95-96.

The Journey Is Our Home

JEANETTE HOLT

In recent years I have become a collector of metaphors and illustrations to help in understanding and describing the changing scene in Baptist life, metaphors to help sort out who we are and what we are becoming. I've used the biblical imagery of exile and lament, poetic metaphors, examples from nature, inscriptions on tombstones, and quotations from historical figures.

One of my favorites is a story about Daniel Boone. When asked if he had ever gotten lost in his travels through the uncharted frontier, Boone replied that he'd been *confused but never lost.* "Once I was confused for three days," he said, "but never lost." I still like that one!

And that story takes me back to the confusion and disorientation many of us in the Southern Baptist Convention felt a decade and more ago when it became clear that the fundamentalist victories within the Southern Baptist Convention were going to be more than just an irritating setback.

I remember quite clearly the first time I heard about the Alliance of Baptists—then called the Southern Baptist Alliance. It was in February 1987, and I was attending a board meeting of the Baptist Peace Fellowship of North America. After two days at Koinonia Farms in South Georgia, we returned to Atlanta for Sunday worship. After lunch we went to the Martin Luther King Center. Copies of the news release announcing the formation of the Alliance were passed around. The statement said the Alliance was not a political organization, would not endorse candidates for office in the SBC or work at getting out the vote. My initial reaction was, "Well, what are they going to do."

I was working for the Baptist Joint Committee on Public Affairs, and even though I was beyond weary of the perpetual battle to survive, it was difficult for me to see the value of any new organization that wasn't going to join in that fight. It took a while for me to understand that our heritage is not dependent on denominational structures and, indeed, is sometimes at greatest risk from those structures.

The events that precipitated the formation of the Alliance were attacks on religious liberty as represented by the Baptist Joint Committee, on the freedom for the word of God especially in seminaries, beginning with organized attacks on faculty and administrators at Southeastern Seminary and on the autonomy of the local church and the priesthood of believers by way of a resolution passed in 1984 that rejected the leadership and calling of women in ministry. Less than six weeks after reading that news release, I joined the Alliance having concluded that not all battles are won or lost at the annual meeting of the Southern Baptist Convention.

When I read the Alliance Covenant I knew that the Alliance represented Baptists at their best. That original covenant declared that we would stand for these principles and exert our influence and channel our ministry "within the Southern Baptist Convention." But as events unfolded, that assertion became increasingly difficult and unproductive.

Let me confess that—in the language of the twelve-step programs—I consider myself a recovering Southern Baptist. I frequently identify myself as a product of the program. I went to it all—at the Gambrell St. Baptist Church in Fort Worth, Texas, one block from Southwestern Baptist Theological Seminary—Sunbeam Band, Girl's Auxiliary, Vacation Bible School, Sunday School, Training Union, G.A. camp, choir, Woman's Missionary Union. If Southern Baptists had a program for it, you name it, we had it, and I went. Wake me from a sound sleep, and I can still quote the GA watchword and the "Star Ideals."

Now in that SBC program I learned a lot: I memorized a lot of scripture, I learned about how we got our Bible, I learned about participatory democracy, I learned to speak in public, and I learned Baptist history and doctrine. I knew a lot about Southern Baptists and almost nothing about any other part of Christ's church, even the other parts of the Baptist family. I have since learned that the world I knew in the South was not necessarily the world experienced by Baptists in the North (where you are hardly ever the majority). That myopia was symbolized for me in my first visit to Valley Forge about six years ago.

A group of Alliance representatives had traveled to the American Baptist headquarters to participate in discussions with representatives of the ABC Task Force on the Southern Baptist Convention. Prior to the formal meetings we were given a tour of the facility. In the resource center our guide pointed out a trunk that had belonged to Adonirum Judson. I thought he was ours! I knew intellectually that Judson's life and ministry came at a time that preceded the severing of our Baptist witness north and south, but on an emotional level this was a powerful reminder that we are truly one family—even when we have allowed time, distance, and disagreement to weaken our connectedness.

For the past thirteen years I have lived in the metropolitan Washington area, working for nearly seven years at the Baptist Joint Committee on Public Affairs and now, for nearly seven years at the Alliance, as a member of University Baptist Church of College Park, Maryland, and involved in the life and ministry of the D.C. Baptist Convention (the only dually-aligned entity in either American Baptist or Southern Baptist structures).

When I first moved to the D.C. area, I had never met an American Baptist; had never heard of the Baptist General Conference, North American Baptists, or Progressive National Baptists, much less Seventh-Day Baptists. I have had the great blessing of being pulled outside my parochial and frequently arrogant assumptions about where and how and through whom God works in this world.

Nostalgia can be the belief that God's creativity has peaked at some time in the past. But God is always calling us to be more than we have been.

That brings me to another metaphor—from the *Washington Post*. William Rasberry, writing about the stress and trauma in Russia and about the sometime confusion of the Clinton administration in regard to its priorities, began a column with a story about his Aunt Bessie.

His aunt was a country woman, said Rasberry. And he described her first experience with a big-city escalator. She watched other department store shoppers mount the contraption for a long time and then finally got up the nerve to try it herself. Not quite ready to make the full commitment though, Rasberry says, she placed one tentative foot on the bottom-most tread while keeping the other on solid ground. In no time at all, of course, she was in a completely ridiculous situation (funny only in retrospect) and screaming "Help!" for all she was worth.

For those of us who got on the escalator with both feet, some time ago, it's difficult not to be impatient with those who still stand at the bottom and gaze at those who can't bring themselves to lift that second foot.

Most of us came into the Alliance, to some extent, as reaction or protest against the abuse of principle, practice, or persons. But we have found within this movement called the Alliance far more than shared outrage or organized resistance. I think what we have found is a strong sense of community internally and a vision of the possibilities in mission, ministry, and reconciliation beyond anything I would have contemplated if I had remained a happy, ignorant, self-satisfied Southern Baptist.

There is so much fragmentation and, not just in among white Baptists in the South, so much work to be done. One of the founders of the Alliance, Alan Neely, put it this way:

> If we are looking for a mission, being a voice for Christ's cause and principles is a mission; standing with the oppressed and the marginalized is a mission; attempting to be a reconciling agent among Baptists and between Baptists and the broader church is a mission; supporting causes that others consider too risky or too controversial is a mission.

That is the vision of the Alliance of Baptists.

Several years ago John Claypool wrote a delightful book called *Glad Reunion.* It is a provocative, fresh look at some of the most familiar men and women in the Old Testament. In talking about Samuel, Claypool reminds us that at the end of his life, living in one of those "hinge eras" in the life of his nation, Samuel recognized that something genuinely new was emerging and that old structures would no longer work. So Samuel changed his mind. He let go of the old and embraced the new.

In ways we never could have anticipated, God is relentlessly wrenching us out of the past and pressing us forward into a future that is shattering to the comfort and familiarity of the status quo. The polarization within our conventions is often much greater than what has historically divided us as American Baptists and Southern Baptists—race, geography, and organizational styles. In a post-denominational era, my hope and prayer is that we will have the courage and vision that Samuel demonstrated—to let go of the old and to embrace the new. It makes all the difference as we face this journey if we view the events of recent years as the workings and possibilities of God rather than as insurmountable tragedy.

Loren Meade of the Alban Institute has done a helpful job of explaining the changing landscape of religious life in America. He says that what congregational and denominational life will come to look like will not be clear in our lifetimes but challenges us to be part of the unfolding of what is needed rather than an impediment to it. It is good to remember, in the words of the Ruth Duck hymn, "the journey is our home"—and I'm grateful for companions like you on that journey.

Confronting the Challenges

ELAINE SMITH

The challenges that face American Baptists are like the challenges that face other denominational groups, both Protestant and non-Protestant. It seems to me that there are three pivotal questions we must confront.

First, why aren't there more people running to the doorsteps of our churches crying, "What must I do to be saved?" Second, for many of those who have come to our church doorsteps, why don't they find the message compelling enough to stay? And finally, for those who stay, in the words of Rodney King, "Why can't we all just get along?" I would be delighted to say that I have the definitive answers to these concerns, but I do not. However, I'd like to suggest some approaches we may take to address these concerns in a manner that is consistent with the teachings of Jesus Christ.

With respect to the first two questions, why aren't more persons coming to our churches and why aren't more people staying in our churches, I am reminded of one of my favorite movies, *The Sound of Music*. In the movie, there is an exchange between the countess and Maria in which the countess tells Maria, "There is nothing more irresistible to a man than a woman who is in love with him." I'd like to suggest that this is not just a male reaction to the knowledge that one is loved, but it is a human reaction. We know when someone loves us and wants to be around us. At the very least, when we are loved in an unconditional and nonjudgmental manner, we believe that those who love us must have good taste. If we want persons to come to our doorsteps, to feel welcome and want to stay once they come, we must show them the open and nonjudgmental love of Jesus Christ. If we are sincere in extending this love, I believe others will come, and they will stay.

As for the third issue of getting along, I'm sure you remember U.S. Air Force F-16 pilot Scott O'Grady who was shot down over Bosnia some time ago. There was much praise for him and his training because of his ability to survive for days on rainwater and insects.

When questioned about the survival training he received, Lieutenant Colonel William Osborne, the deputy commander of the Air Force base survival school that O'Grady attended simply stated, "What we do teach here is: You don't eat the fuzzy bugs."

Unfortunately, ABC is confronting a number of "fuzzy bug" issues, and we will not have the option of eating them or not eating them. These "fuzzy bug" issues such as homosexuality, the disfellowshiping of churches, and the attempt to control the personal lives of the denominational executives and staff, to name a few, are confronting us now. When fuzzy bugs are consumed (dealt with), they can scratch the throat as they are swallowed; they can cause indigestion; they can cause a stomach virus; or, the reaction may be severe enough to cause death to the body as we know it.

In order to deal with these issues, we must focus on the faith that is our common bond and stress tolerance and appreciation for the diversity we bring to the table—for this is the critical element of our American Baptist heritage. If we are to survive the assault of these divisive issues, we must be willing to dialogue about our differences and, if necessary, agree to disagree. Whatever the nature of the discussions, they must be carried out within the expanse of the love of Jesus Christ.

We can't avoid the fuzzy bug issues, but my view of the challenge to ABC is best expressed in a sermon by Margaret Cowden, president of the American Baptist Extension Corporation, in which she says, "I don't believe there is anything *wrong* with American Baptists that cannot be fixed by what is *right* with American Baptists." Please pray with me that, as members of the denomination, we will remember our call and face those issues that come before us in a manner that reflects the teachings of our Lord and Savior, Jesus.

An Everlasting Vision
for an Everchanging View

KATE PENFIELD

These are exciting days for Baptists as we live between hope and terror. The words by which Czech Republic President Vaclev Havel describes the whole world in our age also characterize the world of Baptists: a shifting of the tectonic plates. The equivalent corporate buzz term is "paradigm shift." Underneath the visible and the known the foundation is moving, and the structures we have created upon it are consequently disintegrating or at least changing shape. We who have gathered because we value our Baptist heritage and intend to pass it on are wondering: How shall we live from our Baptist convictions when the familiar ways are in transition?

The futures piece: What is and what is to be, from an American Baptist perspective. We have been reflecting on where we have been as Baptists North and South, who also divide ourselves into a myriad of other categories: liberal and conservative and moderate and fundamentalist, African-American and European-American and Hispanic-American and Native-American and Asian-American; Progressive National, National, Southern, American, Alliance, Cooperative Fellowship; and on and on—you can tell by the ever proliferating and changing names by which we call ourselves that we are far from one and far from secure in our knowledge and trust of each other. At the same time, many of our churches have ceased to call themselves Baptist out of shame for what that name now conjures up. It is no longer good marketing to keep Baptist in your name. Who wants to sign up for a fight?

We therefore know intimately the impasse where today finds us; yet we know also in the depths of our hearts how God would have things be in this world headed toward a destiny where all creation encircles the throne of God, the nearer each in the circle is to sister and brother, the nearer we all are to God. Notice that I said "all creation." Even though we are a long way even from standing side by side as human sisters and brothers, God summons us also to cease from raping and pillaging and oppressing and shutting out any part of this creation named very good, to recognize and honor also earth and animals, lest we all die. Sin that allows us to treat the other as so fundamentally other that we use or abuse or exclude him or her or it is the issue. We call it original sin.

But today we are here to deal with the particularities of the split among God's people called Baptists, a split begun around the particular sin of racism, the aspect of original sin entangled with our roots as nation and church. For the Meeting House of the First Baptist Church in America this conference is a coming full circle, from 1845 when this church was involved in a last-ditch effort to avert the impending split, too little and too late, until today when we have gathered in this space in the hope that perhaps it is now not too late to undo the damage, as a matter of fact just the right time to heal the wounds and be whole.

This is a moment of incomparable opportunity. We stand at the threshold of a new millennium with all its potential to capture the human imagination for new beginnings in a revolutionary thrust toward wholeness, on the anniversary of a split that sunders our hearts because it so tragically moved in the opposite direction, at the point of parenthesis between a modern and a postmodern world.

Everywhere in the world of religion there is an air of crisis, of *kairos* moment aptly summed up by the Chinese characters that represent the word "crisis"—danger and opportunity. There is danger, there is threat, from both within and without traditional religious structures, as everything is in flux from a past that we know all too well to a future that may replicate the worst of the past, or may transcend the known in exciting new shapes we cannot now even imagine—perhaps both. And that, believe it or not, is good news for the likes of us who long for and look for a way beyond the impasse, who are called to play our parts in the transformation, even though we cannot yet discern clearly what those parts will be.

When I first began to prepare for today, the immediate question concerned the principal purpose of this gathering. Have we come together in the hope of addressing and transcending the racism behind the 150-year-old gulf between Baptists north and south, or is our goal simply to find a way beyond that rupture toward intra-Baptist dialogue (not that the latter is simple)? The more I examined the question of goal, the more apparent it seemed that the issues are too entangled to isolate. We Baptists were born in our separate configurations, in fact conceived by, the original sin that then as well as today manifests itself as racism. We have known its other faces, such as sexism, tribalism—a failure to recognize the other as sister or brother. This top-down, hierarchical style must cease.

Part of today's tearing within Baptist bodies arises from the diverging agenda of those who would strive for full partnership of all God's people in the mission of the church, and those who are beginning to say openly in the name of an anti-affirmative action stance that it is time to stop our thrust toward inclusiveness. For many Baptists the tests of fellowship are drawing a very small circle, excluding any churches that would include gays and lesbians, women in ministry, people who have been divorced, seminaries, and the racial-ethnic branch of the family in leadership positions. People who have come out of the SBC will recognize that culture war in the world come into the church to wreak havoc. The drawing of battle lines clarifies the mind and fortifies the soul to stand up and stand for the agenda of Jesus Christ, through whose eyes we recognize all people as sisters and brothers who must stand together.

Consider the poignant hope in the words of Richard Furman, pastor of the First Baptist Church, Charleston, South Carolina, at the 1814 convention in Philadelphia that subsequently became the Triennial Convention, the first national body of Baptists in the United States:

> We have one Lord, one faith, one baptism; why should our ignorance of each other continue? Why prevent us from uniting in one common effort for the glory of the Son of God? At the present convention the sight of brethren [and sisters] who had never met each other before and had never expected to meet on earth, afforded mutual and unutterable pleasure. It was as if the first interviews of heaven had been anticipated.

It reminds me of the sublime moments of recognition when I was privileged to preach in Baptist churches of Cuba and found myself saying over and over as the spirits of congregations seemed literally to leap up to meet mine: "I know you. I recognize you from somewhere, from another dimension, from heaven, from eternity." What is bound in heaven is one already within time, have we but the eyes to see and the spirits open to receive.

Yet what began as mutual and joyous recognition among Baptists in the United States of 1814 disintegrated into acrimonious divorce in 1845. You see, human beings cannot afford to recognize whatever interferes with their primary love, too often materialism—which is a spiritual issue because it has to do with the gods we worship—too often the known and familiar because the change all around as we follow the God who is forever doing a new thing is terrifying. The rupture was a spiritual matter, which shall never be healed unless and until we get at the spiritual roots.

It is likewise a spiritual matter that has yet again divided Southern Baptists and now threatens to balkanize American Baptists. Having been told as I have sought to be a bridge-builder within my own denomination that what happens to bridges is that they get stepped on, my American Baptist spirit certainly resonates with Daniel Vestal's words that describe his efforts to make peace within the SBC a decade ago:

> After a year of sincere effort at being a "man in the middle" reaching out to both sides, I realized that only one side really wanted reconciliation. I realized the Fundamentalists only desired control, total control, absolute control, and that they wanted no participation except with those who had the same desire.

You cannot build a bridge without a foundation on both sides; in fact, bridge-builders, because they stand in the middle trying to hold things together, tend to get stepped on from both sides.

The SBC dilemma I have long known from outside as I sat with groups engaged in ABC-SBC dialogue, watched the Alliance emerge, preached at one of their annual meetings against a divorce fight to the death of the soul over the house they had built, talked with people in tears come here to this Meeting House to touch their roots and weep over the loss of the freedom this place symbolizes, preached at the 1995 Cooperative Baptist Fellowship meeting. Never once did I expect the soul liberty that I have as an American Baptist so taken for granted to be similarly jeopardized.

That is the bad news, but because God is still God, the bad news in fact becomes the good news. In the fellowship room of the First Baptist Church in America Meeting House there is a banner bearing these words: "Behold, I am doing a new thing." The rest of that passage from Isaiah 43:19 you know: "Do you [plural] not perceive it?"

In and through all of our brokenness God is doing a new thing, and people are beginning to perceive and respond as movements toward wholeness have arisen, partly motivated by the economic necessity of finding new ways to accomplish our goals. Everywhere I go I find Baptist people who are speaking the language of partnership as we are pushed by dissension within our bodies to look beyond traditional boundaries for those of like spirit with whom we might do mission.

So what if the shifting of the tectonic plates is shattering the denominations we have known and loved? The fragmentation of artery-hardened national bodies is not necessarily bad news, because their purpose always was simply to mobilize energy and resources for God's mission in the world, and there are ways more suited to our age to accomplish that end, as corporations of all types are discovering. Denominations were never the point; the issue is simply how we can get the job done. And they no more than any other corporate structures are immune from the transformation process going on in the decentralized, diversified, customer-focused, niche-seeking, customized-service, collaborative-style world of today. Hear me well: I am not calling for the death of denominations, because their linking function we shall always need; but I am calling for the perhaps equally painful process of reassessment and transformation.

How can we most effectively carry out God's mission in the name and the way of Jesus Christ? At a macro-level, unprecedented creative overtures are emerging, as exemplified by the 1995 ABC General Board Executive Committee's adoption of a statement called "Partners in Mission," which begins:

> There are many non-American Baptist Churches across the USA who belong to *bona fide* state and national conventions, conferences, or fellowships but hold much in common with the ABC, USA in their understanding of historic Baptist principles and their commitment to the worldwide mission of the church. Whenever possible, feasible, and appropriate, American Baptists must be committed to working together with such churches for the sake of the gospel and in ways which are mutually strengthening.

The document then goes on to lift up existing examples, such as the "Associated Relationship" of the ABC and the Progressive National Baptists since 1970, the recently initiated joint support and staffing of Central Seminary by ABC and CBF, the ABC Ministers and Missionaries Benefit Board servicing of CBF, Alliance, and PNBC staff members and missionaries; it further describes additional explorations in process; and finally it empowers the ABC General Secretary to negotiate the conditions of strategic partnership affiliation with each interested Baptist body.

That same partnership impulse is replicated in infinite ways at the micro-level as people in the places where mission actually occurs are inventing new ways to join forces, and denominational structures themselves are recognizing ever more clearly that congregations sufficiently vital and connected to do mission are the point of the whole enterprise. My itinerary of one two-week period illustrates.

At the beginning of one week I met with people in the Midwest working together to reshape the work of the center on the ministry there to service churches of all descriptions, with focus on congregational vitality instead of the individual career tracks of pastors. Everywhere ecumenical efforts for the empowerment of the laity to discern, decide, and do the work of the church are at the forefront.

In the middle of that week I met with the planning committee for a conference of ABC regional and national staff to focus all our efforts on vital congregations linked for mission in their settings.

At the end of the week when the board of *Baptists Today* met in Atlanta, we discussed broadening that newspaper to systematically report news from the entire Baptist spectrum across the continent. From one end of the country to the other, communication to facilitate networking is another hot item.

The next week in Kansas City, I moderated a dialogue between ABC and CBF church members as they considered how they might work together in reaching out to the considerable needs of their metropolitan area. ABC folk expressed fear of an SBC territorialistic imperative acted out in the prior history of that region; CBF folk wondered if they might be signing up for another fight as they engage in ventures with the ABC facing the same internal struggles they suffered in the SBC; each worried about how to partner a group with such significant style differences; together they concluded that ministry in the name and the way of Jesus Christ requires them to join forces for particular tasks.

CBF and Alliance folk have similar testimonies from the places where they live and move and have their being. These pushes toward partnership are small pieces of the larger picture as new collaborations are springing up everywhere in these times of fragmentation, because we now know definitively that we need each other not to make structures but to do ministry. God is up to something, and we are beginning to recognize one another as essential partners in the process.

Martin Marty recently summed up the dynamic when he addressed the Midwest Career Development Service:

> Leadership needs to work within a consortium, as far as I am concerned. A consortium is a body of people who can't wait. . . . In the midst of the brokenness of the church, they say, "For these functions, let's get together." That's the kind of leadership we're going to need for the church of tomorrow.

In addition to the push toward new partnerships, there is a men's movement going on. The phenomenon known as Promise Keepers has summoned hundreds of thousands of men to fill stadiums for spiritual revivals and a calling to account to live responsible lives. The Million Man March summoned somewhere between 400,000 and a million—the latest figure is 837,000, give or take 20%—African-American men to Washington, D.C., for a similar experience. No matter how we might question the motives and tactics of key organizers, as some have done with both of these movements, they have obviously tapped into a deep hunger in the men of our age who long for togetherness with one another, with God, with their own best selves. God is up to something.

How shall we respond? Unfortunately, too many of the likes of us moderates and progressives are backing away from these newly inspired men, assuming that they have already been co-opted by people with the will to separate into racism and sexism. But listen to the vows that they have made in their mass meetings, to return to their home religious institutions and get involved to improve their communities. I say, let us take them at their word and seek them out, welcome them home, invite them into partnerships for our common mission that is at all our doorsteps. In the name of God, let us not abdicate this opportunity in the assumption that they are not of kindred spirit. Let us not be like elder brothers and sisters sulking in the field. Let us recognize and embrace our brothers as people who may also well be willing to be partners with us to get the job done.

If we believe that God is still God, let us target all of our efforts not on assumptions of dissension and decline and deficit and defeat and death, but on discovering what new things God is up to and who will partner with us in doing God's agenda. Let us not waste precious time and energy and resources on engaging with those eager to fight, but on recognizing whosoever will join us in the work at hand.

On this Reformation weekend, let us embrace the new thing God is doing as we dream of a new reformation for Baptists on this continent, a transcending of denominational lodgings in strategic partnerships. Hear me well: not structural alignments to create a mega-denomination, but spiritual affiliations to do the work. Let us imagine beyond the confines of space and time God's great chess board, on which we exercise our precious freedom to make our moves within the framework of an all-encompassing reality. God, who shall be all in all, who shall be encircled by a creation in harmony, sets the trajectory of our lives within time to draw us together toward the goal, therefore toward one another, joining our missions for the sake of God's mission that this beloved world shall be saved in all the richness of that term: healthy, whole, holy.

I believe that we shall never see the end of our labors in elaborate, static, secure institutions like the ones that shaped our development. While there is a yearning in us to create something permanent for ourselves and as a legacy for those who follow, like the sojourners in the wilderness who lived in temporary shelters as they journeyed, we too dwell in ephemeral structures created by our own hands, always needing to be dismantled and rebuilt as we make our way into a new day. Perhaps the best gift we can pass on to the next generation is a new way of being church together, that more faithfully and effectively and peacefully incarnates God's love to our age, that facilitates the journey because there are no longer cumbersome structures to slow us down.

I further make here a proposal that I make to every Baptist group I am privileged to address: that Baptists by whatever name agree together to celebrate a season of Jubilee, the practice commanded of Israelites every fiftieth year to let their fields lie fallow for renewal, and to forgive debts. Just over the horizon we face a new millennium, in one sense merely an artificial boundary in time, yet also an opportunity to seize imaginations with hope for new beginnings.

I wonder what would happen if Baptists agreed together for a set period of time to cease planning structural changes and preparing resolutions or statements of concern, to stop engaging in those activities that would eventuate in votes and probably fights at our next national gatherings, instead to invest those energies in prayer together, in the expectation that God who is still God is speaking a message about what is to come that we might miss if we are too busy with business as usual. If we truly yearn for God to "shed light on the present day and enable us to begin envisioning a common future that transcends racial, regional, and all other barriers"—as the goal of this conference puts it—here is a place to begin.

Furthermore, our prayers during that time might actually inspire us to the Jubilee mandate of letting the debtors go free, in other words to forgive those who have trespassed against us, to let one another off the hook for the past, to repent and be reconciled. Red and yellow, black and white, fundamentalist and moderate and evangelical and liberal, lay and ordained and denominational leaders, we have much to forgive each other, much that will hinder our entry into a new day. Mutual forgiveness is the only way to proceed together into the future, and that we must do; God cannot do it for us.

A Dorothy Sayers poem said it eloquently: "All things God can do but this one thing: God will not unbind the chain of cause and consequence or speed time's arrow backward." We cannot turn time backward and erase our bitter history, but we can interrupt the cycle by refusing to do unto others what has been done to us. We can search our souls for a way to forgive and go on together.

There is a line in a song that sums up what might bring us together: "An everlasting vision for an everchanging view." If together we set our eyes on the God we have known through Jesus Christ, the changeless good news we see there just might capture our hearts and ignite our spirits to take on tomorrow united. In this upper room of the First Baptist Church in America, we remember not just our Baptist heritage; we also remember another upper room, where the Spirit of God was poured in power to change the world upon people all together in one place, of one accord.

No one of us has the answers to our contemporary dilemmas; they belong to and arise from all of us together. Recognition of each other as sister and brother is the key, discovered when we draw near to God through Jesus Christ and in the light of his story see at last who we truly are. We are able to partner with God in the healing of creation only when we are able to recognize as partners our sisters and brothers who stand beside us. May God give us eyes to see one another as God sees us, so flawed that we need a Savior, so loved that the Son of God has come to live for us and beside us and within us.

On Higher Ground
John 4:1-30

WALLACE CHARLES SMITH

I don't think it comes as a surprise to any of us that there's a great search for meaning going on in all traditions and cultures. A few months ago I saw an old movie from the 1960s that really character-ized the times. It starred Michael Caine and in many ways voiced the "grouplessness" of the 1960s. With its well-known anthem, "What's It All About, Alfie?" it speaks to the deeper issue, the issue of mean-ing. We ask that question all the time: "What is life all about?"

I'm fond of reading bumper stickers. Sometimes bumper stickers can give us a glimpse into our human quest for meaning. I saw one the other day that simply said: "So many pedestrians, so little time." What's it all about, Alfie? More and more the world becomes a place of hostility, people snapping, people hurling insults. Freeways have become places for gestures of all kinds, shapes, and sizes. What's it all about, right now in particular as Congress looks at certain issues affecting the lives of all of us? The economy—according to some, it's getting better; according to others who still can't find work, not bet-ter. Drug epidemics are running unchecked. What's it all about?

This text is an interesting glimpse into the importance of imagery. It says that at high noon Jesus meets a woman at a well in Samaria. Two quests for meaning across cultural divides meet in one dramatic moment. Jesus has become so popular that his baptisms are now more popular than John's, and because of the threat that the power establishment feels, Jesus must retreat from Jerusalem and go back to the friendlier confines of Galilee where he was born and reared. The text says that on his way back to Galilee, "he must needs go through Samaria." Because of his popularity and his own quest for meaning, he is retreating to the place that he knows best and to friends and those who've given him support in the past. But even as he is retreating into a search for deeper meaning, the text says, "He must needs go through Samaria."

Samaria—the place of the hated Samaritans. Those of you who know your history know that the hatred between the Jews and Samaritans was deep. Samaritans and Jews not only didn't see eye to eye; they did not like each other. Their divisions were irreparable. It goes back to the fact that Samaritans were thought by Jews to have been sell-outs during the time of their captivity. The Jews believed that the Samaritans—formerly of the Northern Kingdom under the auspices of the Assyrians—had just been too willing, had gone too easily toward capitulation with their conquerors. The Jews believed that they themselves had held out during their Babylonian captivity. Although they had made some errors, at least they had been true to the faith. So the Jews believed that they had the moral high ground.

There's a line from the musical Carousel that says something like this: "Stonecutters cutting on stone, woodchoppers chopping on wood, there's nothing quite as bad as a man who thinks he's good." This Jewish establishment thought that they had the high ground because they felt that they were good. So on this fatal day, after Jesus and his disciples have gone through the desert, through the thistles and thorns of nothingness, they wind up in this country of Samaria at a city called Sychar.

In this city is a stone well known as "Jacob's Well." As they get to the well, it's high noon—a time in which the sun is at that place where morning is in arrears, and afternoon and evening are still ahead. And here at high noon, Jesus just sits at the well and sends his disciples into the city for provisions—to fill their sacks with some things they can eat and feast upon after this long, hot, dusty trip. The disciples go on to find some Big Macs, some Giants, some Whoppers, and whatever.

Jesus sits at the well. And at the well, meaning intersects with opportunity. And when meaning intersects with opportunity, it's a grace moment. A woman from the city comes to the well, and Jesus sitting there asks her a simple question that in many ways revolution-izes salvation history. He simply says, "Give me a drink of water."

The woman looks at him. You might say she checks him out. She notices from his style of hair that he is a rabbi. She can tell from his dress that he is a teacher. And so she says to him, "You mean, you, a Jew, are asking me, a Samaritan, for a drink of water?" If you unpack this thing for a moment, in effect she is saying, "Come on, man. I've been around a long time. I've heard every line in the book. 'Don't I know you from somewhere? Haven't I seen you somewhere before?'" And in her mind she is saying, "You rabbis are all alike—talk Jew;

sleep Samaritan. Who do you think you are? You mean that you, a Jew, ask me, a Samaritan, for some water?"

Jesus says to her, "If you knew who was asking, then you would have come for water and would have received living water."

The two of them spar back and forth, intellectually jousting. Then she goes on and says, "Well, you have no bucket, and secondly, this well was given to us by our ancestor Jacob. You mean to tell me that you have some water that is superior to what our ancestors provided?"

Jesus says, "If you drink from this well, you never will thirst again."

She says, "Jesus, you don't have a bucket."

She has the bucket. She has the utensils. She has what's necessary.

She says, "I have the bucket, and the well is deep. You tell me you have something I don't have?"

As I read this text, it strikes me that at one level or another in churches—all churches that I have some contact with—an issue is the bucket issue. The bucket issue is that some of us feel that if we have the tools, then we have the substance. So if the sanctuary is magnificent enough, and if the stained glass is artistically sufficient to excite our imaginations, and if the organ is majestic enough and it swells and rises, something inside us lifts.

If we have the tools in order, then we've got the substance. Tool fixation is an issue that I've seen often in many places. It cuts across racial and cultural lines. It's when we think that those outside factors can somehow contribute to inner fulfillment and refreshment. Sometimes we think we have the tools straight, and Lord knows, those of us from the Baptist side of the aisle certainly know that when it comes to the mode of baptism, we have the right tools.

She has the bucket. The well is deep. Because the well is deep, unless the bucket is present, then she cannot get water from the well. But then, she also has the place. She says that this well was given to us by Jacob. The place is significant. This is historic. This is something passed down through generations. This is the place. I've got the tools. This is the place. What else could there be in life?

And Jesus says, "If you drink from this water, you will thirst again. But if you drink from the water that I have before you, then you'll never ever thirst."

Then she moves the conversation on a bit and says, "Then, give me some of that water." You can almost hear the cynicism in her voice. "Give me some of that water." In other words, "Get back, Jack. Give me some of that water because, after all, I'm sick and tired of every day having to come out here and tote water from the well back into the city because you menfolk see that as women's work. And so if I can get this water, that will cause us to never thirst again. Then I can give up this meaningless task and be about the business of doing something more productive."

And when she says that, Jesus moves the conversation to another level. He says, "Fine. Alright. Then go back to the city and bring your husband."

And she says, "Well, uh . . . , I don't have a husband."

And he says, "Yea, that's right because you've had five of them, and the one you're presently with is not your husband."

This woman has had relationships, deep pain, through a lifetime of not being able to establish a meaningful, committed relationship. This woman is struggling for meaning. She thinks she can find it in relationships. Again the bucket issue. How many of us have thought that we could find meaning in relationships, in friendships, in the arms of someone else, and not been able to find it?

When Jesus raises the specter of her deepest pain, the pain of this breach in relationships, then they're ready to talk honestly and openly. Now the jousting is over. Now the sparring has ended. Now they're at the deepest stuff of life. No more masks. No more playing. Now she is talking to Jesus at the soul level.

She says, "But how? How is that possible? If indeed, as you have already said, by looking at my innermost self . . . But there's something in you that perceives beyond what human beings can normally see. And if there's something there—and I perceive it is there—I perceive it is of the Spirit. And your spirit is asking me, a Samaritan, to with you, a Jew, find this living water? But how can that be? It is not possible because my people worship on this mountain, and your people worship in Jerusalem. The reason we have been divided all these years is the whole issue of our mountains. Which mountain, Jesus? If we are going to have living water shared equally, which mountain? Is it your mountain, or is it my mountain?"

Again Jesus begins pushing to show her and to show us what is the bucket issue. Here's a woman who has a bucket, but the bucket has a hole in it. She doesn't realize that, although she is performing the everyday business of doing whatever she needs to do to make it through the day, there's a hole in the bucket.

Living water cannot be carried as long as we are unmindful of the holes in our buckets. Across the span of humanity, there are certainly cracks and fissures, holes in our buckets. Racism—there's a hole in the bucket. Sexism is a hole in the bucket, an unwillingness to allow human beings to define themselves and to claim their own ground. There's a hole in the bucket. The first thing the woman at the well had to do was admit the insufficiency of her equipment. And then Jesus pointed her to the reality.

But equally with the bucket issue is the question of mountain. Which mountain? Which place? Shall it be Methodism? Shall it be the Baptist tradition? Shall it be the world churches where many of the younger people are flocking? Shall it be a return to Roman Catholicism for those whose parents left the church years ago? Shall it be a kind of twentieth-century atheism that worships the idols of materialism? Which mountain?

Then Jesus drives it home. He says, "Those who worship God are not concerned about the location of the mountain."

What brings us to that place is something more than the height of our positions. Those who worship God worship in spirit and in truth. They've gotten beyond those narrow particularities. They no longer are concerned with whether we wear suits and ties to church or whether we come in our jeans. They're not using as a fundamental issue whether we read the Mass in Latin or English. It is not a concern whether we have gospel music sung or the anthems of Europe. That's not the issue. The issue is: there is another place, a higher place, somewhere beyond the physical mountains of life, and that higher place is where living water is found.

It's been so good for us to be here—American Baptists, Progressive National Baptists, Alliance of Baptists, Cooperative Baptist Fellowship types, and others—because we have seen that there is another mountain, a higher place than our traditions, a higher place than even our most celebrated pasts.

When the woman understood the truth, the disciples came back and saw Jesus talking to her. They didn't even ask him anything. They didn't know what was going on, but she put down her bucket and went running back to the city, crying, "Come see a man." She thought that she needed the bucket, but found out that her bucket had a hole in it. And then the Master moved into a place to see where these holes and fissures and cracks will never be adequately and completely fixed.

All of us will always have some issues to work through. So we got to get past the bucket as the issue and see that there's only one uniting power, and that is Christ, the Spirit of the Living God, the Spirit that brings the best out of humanity. That's the high mountain.

The woman said, "I perceive that you are the Messiah. I've seen in you something beyond my pain and my brokenness. I've seen in you something greater than all of the lonely nights and all of the insincere arms. I've seen something more important than trying to have relationships with men who have denied me my being and have reduced me to an inanimate object. I have seen in you something higher than what life has given me before. I have seen a place where I can be myself, where I, a Samaritan woman, can drink from the living water from which you, a Jew, can drink; and the two of us together can find something greater in the Spirit of God."

Wouldn't this world be a wonderful place if we could give up our position fixations and our bucket issues and move to that higher ground? I think that's what Isaiah talked about. He said, "Every valley shall be exalted. Every crooked place shall be made straight. Every rough place shall be made plain. The glory of the Lord shall be revealed, and all flesh—all flesh—shall see it together."

Let me share a story with you. Some years ago when I was in Chester, Pennsylvania, we had the Chester Community Improvement Project. It was a partnership of Swarthmore College and some local churches. We got together with volunteers and were redoing houses. Mind you, we were doing this before Jimmy Carter and Habitat for Humanity. Jimmy Carter stole the idea from us! I'll never forget a moment when we turned our first house over to a single woman and two children living right at the poverty level. There was a Roman Catholic priest who was part of our team, a Presbyterian, an African-American minister, myself, some deacons from our church, and students from Swarthmore—most of whom I believe were of Jewish background. We stood there, about ten of us in a circle, and prayed. Father O'Callahan, the Roman Catholic priest, led us in prayer. After the prayer, we turned the key over to that woman who for so many years had been suffering. She cried, and Father

O'Callahan cried, and I cried. After awhile, all of us were crying. The only way I can describe it is at that moment, those of us in that circle and in that room had found a higher mountain than any of our traditions. Regardless of our backgrounds and our denominations, at that moment, at that place, we had experienced the presence of God. Jesus said, "Those who come will worship in spirit and in truth."

Contributors

William H. Brackney
Professor, McMaster University
Principal, McMaster Divinity College
Hamilton, Ontario

Edwin S. Gaustad
Professor Emeritus, University of California
Riverside, California

Stan Hastey
Executive Director, Alliance of Baptists
Washington, D.C.

Jeanette Holt
Associate Director, Alliance of Baptists
Washington, D.C.

J. Stanley Lemons
Professor, Rhode Island College
Providence, Rhode Island

Bill J. Leonard
Dean, Divinity School, Wake Forest University
Winston-Salem, North Carolina

Dwight M. Lundgren
Minister, First Baptist Church in America
Providence, Rhode Island

Thomas R. McKibbens
Pastor, First Baptist Church
Newton Centre, Massachusetts

Kate Penfield
Executive Director, Ministers Council
American Baptist Churches USA
Valley Forge, Pennsylvania

Elaine Smith
President, American Baptist Churches
Washington, D.C.

Wallace Charles Smith
Pastor, Shiloh Baptist Church
Washington, D.C.

0117